Images of War

GREAT WAR FIGHTER ACES 1916-1918

Norman Franks

Pen & Sword
AVIATION

First published in Great Britain in 2017 by
PEN & SWORD AVIATION
an imprint of
Pen & Sword Books Ltd,
47 Church Street,
Barnsley,
South Yorkshire,
S70 2AS

A CIP record for this book is available from the British Library.

ISBN 978 1 47386 126 8

Pen & Sword Books Ltd incorporates the Imprints of
Pen & Sword Aviation, Pen & Sword Maritime,
Pen & Sword Military, Wharncliffe Local History, Pen & Sword Select,
Pen & Sword Military Classics and Leo Cooper.

For a complete list of Pen & Sword titles please contact
Pen & Sword Books Limited
47 Church Street, Barnsley, South Yorkshire, S70 2AS, England

E-mail: enquiries@pen-and-sword.co.uk
Website: www.pen-and-sword.co.uk

Contents

Introduction   5

Chapter 1 – The War Becomes More Serious   7

Chapter 2 – Arras and Bloody April   27

Chapter 3 – New Aeroplanes, New Tactics   51

Chapter 4 – The Winter of 1917-18   75

Chapter 5 – 1918   101

Photographs

As in the first part of this coverage of the aces of the First World War, photograph images have come from many people and many sources over my fifty years of study of First World War flying. Many came from the collections of the pilots themselves, many of whom I had the privilege to either meet or correspond with. Sadly they are now all gone.

Over the years I have co-operated and shared images with a number of friends who also study this period, some of them fellow authors. Some of them too have now departed. The main contributors therefore are, or have been: Greg van Wyngarden, Andy Thomas, Trevor Henshaw, Stuart Leslie, Tony Mellor-Ellis, Walter Pieters, and the late Mike O'Connor, Chaz Bowyer, Frank Cheesman, Ed Ferko, Neil O'Connor, Frank Bailey, Les Rogers and Hal Giblin.

Chapter 1
The Air War Becomes More Serious

In the first part of this two-part series, covering 1914-1916, we ended 1916 as the massive Somme offensive had finally petered out and the German fighter force had established their *Jagdstaffeln*. It will be remembered that in the initial stages of the First World War fighter aeroplanes such as the Fokker Eindeckers, had been distributed in twos and threes amongst the two-seat observation and bombing *abteilungen*, for protection. In between such protection sorties, the more aggressive young pilots had flown their fast little scouts to engage Allied machines that were either ranging artillery fire over the front lines, or flying into German-held territory to observe or bomb.

Two of these pilots had been Oswald Boelcke and Max Immelmann, and both had been the first airmen to receive the coveted *Orden Pour le Mérite*, Germany's highest bravery award. Immelmann had been killed in June 1916 and Boelcke in October, but Boelcke had persuaded 'higher authority' to gather the fighters into a number of single units – *Jagdstaffeln* – shortened to the word *Jasta*.

By this time there were dozens of eager young pilots clambering to become *Jasta* pilots, and emulate the achievements of men such as Boelcke, Immelmann, Wintgens and Berthold. They also sought the recognition these early aces had achieved, as well as high awards from the various German states who all seemed compelled to lavish medals and orders on these new heroes of the skies.

It was not, however, any form of guarantee of a long life, and many of the early aces had already fallen. By January 1917 the three living top-scoring aces were *Rittmeister* Manfred von Richthofen with eighteen victories, *Leutnant* Wilhelm Frankl, with fourteen and *Leutnant* Walter Höhndorf with twelve. The winter weather had curtailed aerial activity to some extent, but the spring was coming, and the *Jasta* pilots were waiting.

On the British side, the DH.2 and FE.8 pusher-type fighters that had helped overcome the Fokker menace were about to be phased out, replaced by tractor-engined machines, there being no need to have engines behind the pilot now that interrupter gears had been invented. The poor BE.12s too were ordered away from the front by no less a personage than General Hugh Trenchard, head of the RFC. December 1916 saw the first Sopwith Pups arrive in France, nimble little single-seat fighters with a single Vickers gun firing through the propeller, and in January 1917 came a newer type of fighting reconnaissance aeroplane, another Sopwith design, the unusually named 1½ Strutter, so called because of its unusual arrangement of the central bracing that supported the upper wing. It too carried a single Vickers gun for the pilot atop the forward fuselage, and also a moveable Lewis gun mounted on a Scarff ring in the rear cockpit. The Strutter could generally handle itself when scrapping with German fighters, and was also used for both short and long reconnaissance missions. The big FE.2bs and 2ds were still very much in evidence and were not attacked without care and attention by the German pilots.

Fighters with the Royal Naval Air Service had for some months been helping to support their RFC comrades, several squadrons taking turns to move down from the North Sea coast area to support the hard-pressed British front. They too had begun to equip with Pups, and Strutters, but were also using French Nieuport Scouts, as the RFC had also been flying. Among the high-scoring British pilots still alive as 1917 began were the mercurial Albert Ball, with thirty-one victories, although he was back in England at this time. E. O. Grenfell had eight, J. O. Andrews seven and S. H. Long, six; J. D. Latta, had five although he was no longer in France. In the RNAS, R. S. Dallas had claimed six, including two flying the new Sopwith Triplane that this Australian was trialling in France. However, the best results went to his fellow Australian, S. J. Goble, who had scored eight by this time, flying Nieuports and Pups. In fact he scored the Pup's first kill in the war, downing a German two-seater on 24 September 1916, which brought him the Distinguished Service Cross.

On the French Front, their fighter aircraft were the Nieuport Scout and Spad VII. Georges Guynemer and Charles Nungesser were the two leading lights, with twenty-five and twenty-one victories. In addition, Guynemer had been credited with four probables.

The French system of crediting aerial victories was, on the face of it, more stringent than the RFC's. Unless an enemy aircraft was seen to crash – and be witnessed by two other sources – it was only noted as probably destroyed and not included in the pilot's score of victories. Similarly, an opponent who was only seen to spin away out of sight, or into cloud, was also only noted as a probable. An enemy in flames, or where the pilot jumped out, also had to be verified by witnesses. The British system of course added probable victories (recorded as 'out of control') to a pilot's overall score. The French system could not have been always as stringent as it might seem, but it was the system. Early French aces still alive as 1917 began were:

René Dorme	17 (and 6 probables)
Alfred Heurtaux	16 (and 3 probables)
Jean Navarre	12 (before seriously wounded, 17 Jun 1916)
Andre Chainet	10 (no longer at the Front)
Albert Deullin	10
Marcel Vialet	9
Jean Chaput	8
Paul Sauvage	8 (and 4 probables; killed 7 Jan 1917)
Paul Tarascon	8
Georges Flachaire	7
Jean Casale	6
Lucien Jailler	6
Victor Sayaret	6
Joseph de Bonnefoy	5

To this list must be added Gervais Raoul Lufbery, French by birth but adopted by America due to having an American father. Born in 1885, at Chamalières, central France, he ran away from home when aged 17 in order to travel the world, even travelling to the USA in 1906, where, after joining the army, he spent two years on active duty in the Philippines. He saw his first aeroplane in Cochin China in 1910, then, making the acquaintance of a French pilot, Marc Poupe, in 1912, began to travel with him as a mechanic. Not long after the war began Poupe was killed and, having returned to France with him, Lufbery had to join the French Foreign Legion due to his US status. His desire to fly led him to becoming a pilot, and when the *Escadrille Lafayette* was formed from American volunteers, he joined them. By the end of 1916 he had shot down six German aircraft, the unit's top ace.

The French had also begun to group *escadrilles* together, starting in October 1916 with *Groupe de Combat 11*, followed by *GC12*. There is no suggestion that each *escadrille* within these groupings acted together: it was more a grouping for administration and ease of command. Further *Groupes de Combat* followed during 1917.

* *

So, as 1917 began, the air war, although stalled by the weather, was about to erupt in earnest. Enough had been learnt during 1916, especially following the Somme battles. The new German *Jasta* pilots were busily training on their new biplane fighters, the Albatros D.I and D.II, Fokker D.I and D.II, that had begun to appear in late 1916 and the LFG Roland D.II that would arrive in the spring. Meantime, the Halberstadt D.II had all but gone from the front, and the Fokker biplanes were also being replaced by Albatros Scouts.

Also in the spring the RFC would receive its first squadron of Bristol F.2a two-seat reconnaissance fighters. This was 48 Squadron, which arrived in March; its senior flight commander was Captain William Leefe Robinson VC, famous for having shot down a German airship over London.

During the first weeks of 1917 there had been some thirty *Jastas* created and formed, many ready for action. Compared to British or French squadrons they had fewer pilots and aircraft, but the aircraft were mostly Albatros D.II or D.III fighters, with a few Fokker or Halberstadt biplanes that were more than capable of inflicting serious damage on most of the Allied aircraft now at the front. Although *Jasta* 2 had lost its formidable leader, Oswald Boelcke, *Oberleutnant* Stefan Kirmaier had taken over but he too had been killed in November by J. O. Andrews of 24 Squadron who had been in the fight when Boelcke had died. As a mark of respect, *Jasta 2* had become known as *Jasta* Boelcke. *Hauptmann* Franz Walz was now its *Staffelführer* .

However, the *Jasta* had lost one of its leading lights, Manfred von Richthofen, in January 1917. He had been promoted to lead *Jasta 11*, and under his leadership it was to become the second highest scoring *Jasta* in the German Air Service. *Jasta 11* had not scored any victories by this time, but the Baron changed this on 23 January, claiming his own seventeenth kill.

It is not always appreciated that the Sopwith Aviation Company built aeroplanes for the Royal Naval Air Service and only later did the RFC begin to order their aircraft. Both the two-seat Sopwith 1½ Strutter and the Sopwith Pup began their service lives in 1916 and by 1917 were used in large numbers by both services. Both were nice to fly. The Strutter pilots had a single Vickers gun atop the forward section of the fuselage, while the observer in the rear cockpit had a drum-fed Lewis gun, mounted on a Scarff ring that enabled it to be swung in various directions. The observer also had extra drums in his cockpit. One can see a gun-sight on the pilot's gun and his windscreen has a leather reinforced edge to avoid facial damage in a forced landing. This particular machine was used by 43 Squadron, and was brought down by *OfStv* Edmund Nathanael of *Jasta 5* on 28 April 1917, his twelfth victory, its crew being captured.

The Sopwith Pup became the standard fighter for both the RNAS and RFC and was once described as a nice 'club machine', meaning it had few vices and did not give its pilot too much trouble. It too had just one single belt-fed Vickers gun for its pilot. This picture of the prototype, 3691, was taken at the Dunkirk Air Depot in May 1916. It then flew with several RNAS units in France including 1 Naval Squadron, where F/Sub-Lt S. J. Goble claimed a German two-seater 'out of control' in September.

Sopwith Pup A626, of 8 Naval Squadron, shot down by Lt Friedrich Mallinckrodt of Jasta 6 on 4 January 1917, for his second victory. He is seen here with his leather flying coat. Severely wounded in April 1917 with Jasta 20, he survived the war as a test pilot, but was killed during the Second World War. He had achieved six victories, although he was wounded on five occasions.

Lt E. O. Grenfell had achieved eight victories by the end of 1916 flying Morane Scouts with 1 Squadron and Nieuports with 60. Circling his last victim, brought down inside Allied lines on 11 December, he crashed and broke a leg. Later he commanded 23 Squadron, was awarded the AFC, and ended the war with the MC. Post-war he won the DFC. He is seen here sitting in front of a French Caudron.

Lt R. S. Dallas DSC ended 1916 with six victories flying with the RNAS. In 1917 he gained sixteen more, mostly with 1 Naval Squadron. From Queensland, Australia, he was among the top-scoring Aussies of the First World War, although sadly he did not survive the conflict. Reggie Dallas received a DSO and a Bar to his DSC, and is here standing in front of a Nieuport 11. He was variously known as Reggie, Stan and 'Breguet'.

The prototype Sopwith Triplane (N500) in which Dallas scored two victories while testing the type for operational evaluation. The Triplane saw considerable service during 1917, and its three-wing design was noted by the Dutch aircraft designer, Anthony Fokker, which led to him building the famed Fokker Dr.I Triplane for the German Air Service.

Another Australian in the RNAS was F/Sub-Lt S. J. Goble, from Victoria. By the end of 1916 he had achieved eight victories and been awarded the DSC and later a DSO. His combat successes came whilst flying both the Nieuport Scout and the Sopwith Pup machines. He later rose to air vice-marshal in the RAAF.

Captain J. O. Andrews of 24 Squadron came from Lancashire and served in the Royal Scots before joining the RFC. Flying the DH.2 he scored seven victories by the end of 1916 and in 1917, with 66 Squadron on Pups, shot down a further five German aircraft. He was awarded the MC and Bar, followed by a DSO. He ended the war commanding a Sopwith Camel squadron, retiring from the RAF as an air vice-marshal.

John Andrews seated in his Sopwith Pup, B1703, in which he claimed his last three victories while with 66 Squadron. The picture was taken at Vert Galant aerodrome, France.

...t Charles Nungesser flew with *Escadrille N65* in 1916 ...nd by the end of that year had twenty victories in air ...ombat. He had won the *Médaille Militaire* with the ...rmy and became a *Chevalier* of the *Legion d'Honneur*. ...le would more than double this score by the summer ...f 1918. However, he suffered a number of wounds and ...njuries during his service, but also received the British ...lilitary Cross, the *Croix De Guerre* (eventually with ...wenty-eight *Palmes* and two *Étoiles* (stars)), and the ...merican DSC. He is seated in a Nieuport Scout with ...is famous personal insignia of a black heart, edged in ...vhite, a coffin, two candlesticks, and a skull and ...rossbones (funereal symbols, to be seen in many old ...hurches).

René Dorme ended 1916 with seventeen victories flying with one of the *Storke Group, Escadrille N3*. When the war began he had been with the French artillery in North Africa, but immediately requested pilot training as he returned to France. He continued to score in 1917, his total reaching twenty-three by mid-May, but was killed in action on the 25th, shot down by Heinrich Kroll of *Jasta 9* for his fifth victory. Dorme recorded more than a dozen probables.

Heinrich Kroll of *Jasta 9* shot down Dorme on 25 May 1917 for his fifth victory. In July he took command of *Jasta 24*, raising his score to 33 by August 1918 when a wound ended his combat career. He received the *Pour le Mérite* in March 1918.

Lt Jean Chaput, of *N57*, had a victory score of eight by the end of 1916. He would down more in 1917 and 1918 before falling in combat in May 1918. Paris-born Chaput had earlier been in the army but transferred to aviation when war began.

It was not just the Germans who had postcards of their heroes. Here *Adjutant* Andre Chainat is depicted by the photographer N. Manuel, in his *'Les As'* series. Seriously wounded after his eleventh victory, he did not return to combat flying. He flew with *N3*, depicted in this picture by the Stork emblem above his medals. These medals are the *Legion d'Honneur*, *Médaille Militaire* and the *Croix de Guerre*, showing eight *Palmes* and two *Étoiles*.

Three early French aces, Alfred Heurtaux, Georges Flachaire and Marcel Vialet of the *Storke Group*. Heurtaux had sixteen victories by the end of 1916 and downed five more before being badly wounded in May 1917. Flachaire ended 1916 with seven victories and gained one more in 1917 before being sent to America as part of the French Military Aviation Mission. Vialet ended his combat career in December 1916 with nine victories.

Four more stalwart *Storke Group* pilots. Mathieu Tenant de la Tour had eight victories in 1916, one more in 1917, but was killed in a flying accident in December 1917. Alfred Heurtaux, Albert Deullin, ten victories by the end of 1916, raised his total to twenty by May 1918; he was killed in a flying accident in 1923. Georges Guynemer, again showing the *N3* Stork emblem

One of the Spad VII fighters used by Guynemer. Again we see the Stork emblem of *Escadrille N3*. Each *escadrille* in the group carried a Stork emblem, but in different designs. Beneath the exhaust pipe is written *Vieux Charles*, the name carried on all of his Nieuport and Spad aircraft. The number '2' is in red. Note the RNAS Sopwith Triplane in the background.

The top ace and French hero of the *Escadrille Lafayette*, Roual Lufbery. His decorations are the *Legion d'Honneur*, *Médaille Militaire*, and *Croix de Guerre* with four *Palmes*. Usually the award of a *Palme* denoted a mention in French communiqués for some feat of distinction.

Lt Walter Höhndorff flew mostly with *Kek* Vaux in 1916 (*Kampfeinsitzerkommando*, based at Vaux airfield). Awarded the *Pour le Mérite* in July, he joined two of the new *Jastas*, 1 and 4, bringing his score to twelve. Later he took command of *Jasta 14* but was killed testing an **AEG D.I**, which he had helped design, on 5 September.

Wilhelm Frankl ended 1916 with fifteen victories, having earlier flown Fokker Eindeckers before going to the new *Jasta 4*. Awarded the *Pour le Mérite* in August, he brought his score to twenty in early April 1917, including four on the 6th, before falling in combat with 48 Squadron's **BF.2a** fighters on 8 April.

The 'Eagles' of von Richthofen's *Jasta 11* in 1917. L to R: Wolfgang Plüschow, Constantin Kempf, Georg von Hantlemann, Kurt Wolff, Karl Effers, von Richthofen, brother Lothar von Richthofen, Hans Hintsch, Otto Brauneck, *Leutnant* Matthof, and Karl Allmenröder.

Another Frenchman who would end the war with nineteen victories was Henri Hay de Slade, who saw action with *N86* in 1917-18 and as commander of *Spa159* in 1918. He began the war in the army but learned to fly in 1916. He died in 1979, aged 86.

The German victory cup, presented to an airman upon achieving his first victory in air combat.

Ray Collishaw's Triplane which he used with 10 Naval in 1917, and in which he scored eighteen victories. His was named *Black Maria*, a name written just below the cockpit.

Once the Sopwith Triplane was phased out, the RNAS squadrons used the Sopwith Camel. This picture is of Fred Banbury's B6230; he flew in 9 Naval, and in this aircraft accounted for five of his eleven victories. This Canadian died on the day the RAF was formed, 1 April 1918, crashing shortly after take-off, possibly due to a heart attack.

Four stalwarts of 3 Naval, Ed Pierce (9), Edwin Hayne (15), Art Whealy (27) and Harold Beamish (11). All survived the war, although Hayne, a South African, died in a flying accident in April 1919. Pierce came from England, Whealy from Canada, and Beamish from New Zealand.

Another successful **RNAS** pilot was Harold Stackard, who flew with 9 Naval in 1917, achieving fifteen victories. Despite his record he was not decorated and became an instructor in 1918. Born in Norwich, he was living in North London in 1914. He died in 1949.

Belgian ace Willy Coppens at the start of his career, seated in a Nieuport Scout. The insignia, in blue, is the insignia of *1ère Escadrille*. He did not begin to score victories until he flew Hanriot HD.1 fighters with *9ème Escadrille* from March 1918.

An exceptional British ace was Captain Philip Fullard DSO MC and Bar. Flying Nieuport Scouts with No. I Squadron he achieved forty victories between May and November 1917. His career was ended by breaking a leg in a football match. The American on the right is Captain Earl 'Win' Spencer Jr, a US Navy aviator, husband to Wallis Simpson, who married the Duke of Windsor in 1936. Fullard died in 1984.

Kurt Erwin Wüsthoff joined the army aged sixteen and learned to fly but was too young for front-line duty and so became an instruc In 1915 he flew bombers in Bulgaria, Ruman and Greece before finally getting to France fighter pilot, with *Jasta* 4. By November 1917 had scored twenty-six victories, adding one more in March 1918. He was awarded the Bl Max and assigned to the staff of *JGI*. Given command of *Jasta 15* he was shot down and taken prisoner on 17 June. In July 1926 he w badly injured in a crash in Dresden and died five days later.

Joseph Veltjens was another ace who began service with the army prior to moving to aviation in late 1915. Via the two-seater route, he eventually made fighter pilot in March 1917, going to *Jasta 14*. In Augus he transferred to *Jasta 18* and later *Jasta 15*. With nine victories by the end of 1917, this rose to thirty-five by October 1918, and had brought him the Blue Max and other high awards. In the Second World War he attained the rank of *Oberst* (colonel) but was killed in October 1943. He was travelling in a Ju52 transport aircraft that was shot down by Yugoslav partisans and he was killed. He was known as 'Seppl'.

Chapter 2
Arras and Bloody April

The beginning of 1917, with its winter weather, kept things fairly quiet on the Western Front. Whenever possible, the reconnaissance aircraft would brave the severe cold to observe either side of the lines and take photographs when conditions were favourable, while the fighter pilots attempted interceptions and maintained patrols.

On the German side it had become policy to await the arrival of either British or French aircraft crossing into their territory. Frontline observers would quickly telephone back, giving information about these incursions, while usually on the airfields closer to the front, observers, by using telescopes on tripods, could actually see for themselves any aircraft crossing over and be able to formulate a plan of action to intercept. It was their way of fighting the air war, whereas the French and particularly the British always took the war to the enemy.

The observation squadrons were still equipped with outdated types that were 'easy meat' for the new German fighters. A whole variety of BE.2 machines carried out a myriad of duties, helped by the better FE.2b and FE.2d aircraft. A new aeroplane had started to arrive, the RE.8, to take on some duties, especially artillery observation (directing fire) and this would gradually replace the BE machines in France. It was better, but the name it acquired – the Flaming Coffin – hardly helped aircrew confidence.

Both sides knew that spring would bring fresh battles, and both were preparing offensives. The new Bristol Fighter squadrons were eagerly waiting to get to grips with the enemy, but the tactics they were busily perfecting would only be proven in actual combat. The new SE.5 was showing promise and one had already been flown to France for evaluation. No. 56 Squadron in England was preparing to take them to France as soon as possible, but this did not happen until 7 April. One of its flight commanders was none other than Captain Albert Ball DSO MC, although he was not really happy with the new type, much preferring the Nieuport Scout. Such was his standing that he was even allowed to have one for his personal use.

On the British side the commanders were preparing for a mighty offensive along a 100-mile section of the Western Front between Arras in the north and the Aisne river in the south. If successful, the British would push forward from Arras, while the French would make their assault from the southern end. On the air side, the RFC would have to start things still equipped with DH.2s and FE.2s, and a few squadrons of Pups. The RFC had also one squadron of French Spad VIIs, and of course the BF.2a unit. There was support from the RNAS with their Pups, Nieuports and Triplanes, while the French had Nieuports and Spad VIIs. General Trenchard knew that while his airmen had wrested a tentative air superiority during and following the Somme battles it was doubtful if this could be maintained now the Germans' new fighter force was just waiting for its chance.

As the Battle of Arras loomed Trenchard had twenty-five squadrons along the chosen battle area, and some 365 serviceable aircraft, about one third being fighters. Opposite, the Germans had an estimated 195 aircraft, of which around half were fighters.

Thursday 5 April saw 48 Squadron fly its first O.P. – Offensive Patrol. Six BF.2a machines took off at around 10.00am, led by Captain Robinson and gained height. Across the lines, Manfred von Richthofen's *Jasta 11* had been alerted and lifted off from their airfield in their Albatros scouts. As would be discovered later in the Bristol's successful air war it was a machine in which the two-man crew could dogfight their opponents, the pilot being able to concentrate on an adversary ahead, while his observer was more than able to protect their rear with his moveable Lewis gun. However, the tactic that had been practised was to close up into a tight formation while the observers maintained a protective field of fire as the formation moved forward. This played into the German pilots' hands and they were able to engage and eventually split up the Bristol formation. The Baron shot down two, Sebastian Festner brought down Robinson, while Georg Simon forced down a fourth. It was a disastrous start, and later Richthofen reported that nobody should fear tackling this new type at the front.

There was some bitter air fighting that first week of April, and on the 8th, Easter Sunday, it was clear from all the activity and artillery fire that a British attack was imminent. No. 48 Squadron was again in the action in the early afternoon, getting into a fight with *Jasta 4*. One Bristol was shot down by Otto Bernert of *Jasta B*, for his sixteenth victory, but the British crews got a bit carried away, claiming six Albatros D.IIIs shot down 'out of control', no fewer than five by Captain D. M. Tidmarsh and his observer Second Lieutenant C. B. Holland. Only one Albatros was lost, but it was flown by Wilhelm Frankl of *Jasta 4*; his machine broke up in the air.

Easter Monday, 9 April, saw the battle begin. Intensive shelling began at midnight, the general signal that something big was about to happen. At 5.30am whistles blew, bayonets were fixed and the soldiers went 'over the top'. Amidst wind and snow showers, and through the smoke of battle, the troops moved forward. In the air Allied aircraft flew in support. No. 48 Squadron once more were in action, losing one machine, but the crews claimed two two-seaters destroyed, one Albatros destroyed with another two-seater and two scouts 'out of control'. Captain A. M. Wilkinson received the DSO for his part in these actions.

Strangely, the German fighters only made a single claim on the 9th, the fourteenth victory for Karl Schäfer of *Jasta 11*. They made up for it on the 11th with nineteen claims, including another for Schäfer, *Jasta 11* once again punishing 48 Squadron, which lost three more aircraft. Lothar von Richthofen shot down one for his second victory, while Kurt Wolff's claim was his ninth. A second RFC Spad squadron had arrived, No. 23, and it lost one machine this day, to *Leutnant* Hermann Frommherz of *Jasta B*, his first victory. Frommherz would end the war with thirty-two victories. He was nominated for the 'Blue Max' but the war ended before it could be awarded.

One Canadian RNAS Pup pilot had a lucky escape. Joe Fall's engine stopped during an air battle and he was forced to land inside German territory. Fortunately, he was able to get his engine going again before anyone came to take him prisoner, so he took off and returned home. Fall, from British Columbia, had gained his first victory on 6 April, and on this day (11th) had claimed three Albatros D.IIs 'out of control' before his engine had quit. Flying Pups and later Camels he would end 1917 with thirty-six victory claims and had received the DSC and two Bars.

Friday the 13th was a really unlucky day for the RFC: 48 Squadron lost another crew; no fewer than six RE.8s were shot down and seven FE.2bs were lost with most of their crews. It was fast becoming what the Americans might call 'a turkey shoot' for the *Jasta* pilots. With their airfields not too far back from the front lines, and targets aplenty in the air over the trenches and across them, the *Jasta* pilots had no lack of opportunities to strike, and strike when it was to their advantage.

The Nieuports of 60 Squadron ran into the grinder on the 14th, *Jasta 11* shooting down four of them. Both Richthofen boys got one each, Festner another, his eleventh, Wolff his fourteenth. That evening the *Jasta* shot down four more, an FE, an RE.8, a Spad and a Pup. Schäfer got the first two, Wolff the Spad and Lothar von Richthofen the Pup.

Observation kite balloons were constantly aloft, their one or two-man crews huddled in a basket beneath the gas-bag, observing movements across the lines, be they troop movements, artillery positions, even motorised transport moving up. They were tempting targets for the fighter pilots, but highly dangerous to attack. While they were defenceless in themselves, they were always surrounded by machine guns on the ground and, more often than not, had fighters patrolling nearby for protection. Some fighter pilots refused to have anything to do with them, while others seem to become fixated by them. If shot down they would be added to a pilot's score of victories, which in itself became something of an incentive.

Heinrich Gontermann of *Jasta 5*, had brought down his first balloon on 8 April, as his eighth kill, another falling to him on the 13th. On the 16th he shot down two and added at least one more by the end of the month. Before his death in an accident on 30 October 1917, he had achieved thirty-nine victories, seventeen of which had been balloons.

Another pilot in *Jasta 5*, Kurt Schneider, shot down three balloons in April. On the 23rd he had claimed three RFC aircraft brought down. In the morning he shot down an FE.2b, but that evening he had attacked several British aircraft, his presence causing a DH.2 and another FE.2b to collide and go down. Having gained a total of fifteen victories by the end of May 1917, his luck suddenly and totally ran out. On 5 June he was wounded in a scrap with an FE.2b of 22 Squadron, crewed by Captain C. E. Clement and Lieutenant L. G. Davies, although he managed to get down safely, but he did not recover, eventually dying from blood poisoning in a field hospital on 14 July. Carleton Clement, from Toronto, achieved fourteen victories with his various observers and was awarded the French *Croix de Guerre*. No doubt he would have been in line for a Military Cross had he not been killed, shot down by AA fire, on 19 August 1917. He was the most successful pilot on the squadron at this time and General Trenchard sent a telegram to the squadron regretting the news of his loss.

No. 60 Squadron had another severe mauling on 16 April, losing four of its pilots, at least three of them falling to *Jasta 11*, Lothar, Wolff and Festner. The Baron shot down a BE.2 in the afternoon, his forty-fifth victory. It was also his *Jasta*'s fifty-sixth claim of the month.

* *

Bad weather reduced aerial activity at this time, but on the 21st, the Pups of 3 Naval Squadron claimed two Albatros Scouts and a two-seater. One was shared between F. D. Casey and H. S. Broad, with H. G. Travers claiming the other. The two-seater went to J. J. Malone, a Canadian. This was John Malone's fifth victory, a score he would double before the month was out, although sadly he was killed on the 30th, shot down by Paul Billik of *Jasta 12*, his first victory. Billik would go on to achieve a score of thirty-one by August 1918. Malone would receive the DSO before he died, and had the rare experience of landing beside one of his victories. On the 24th he forced a DFW two-seater to land inside Allied lines, and so decided to inspect his kill. He found the pilot wounded and the observer dead.

The other three Naval pilots were all achieving success. Francis Casey, from Ireland, shared the downing of Malone's DFW, and by early May had nine victories and had been rewarded with the DSC. Tragically he was killed in a flying accident in a Camel in August. Hubert Broad gained a couple of victories before being wounded in the mouth. He had turned his head to watch an approaching German fighter, and a bullet went into his open mouth and out of one cheek. He later became Chief Test Pilot for the de Havilland Aircraft Company. Herbert 'Tiny' Travers, from London, also shared in Malone's victory, which was his own fifth. He received the DSC. Although he learned to fly pre-war, he had served as a machine-gunner early in the conflict. Post-war he became a test pilot for the Blackburn Aircraft Company, and later an instructor for various flying clubs.

The pilots of 3 Naval were to feature again on 23 April, claiming three Albatros Scouts destroyed and five out of control. Casey was again in evidence and so too was Joe Fall. A. W. Carter claimed two, H. S. Kerby two also, L. Breadner and A. T. Whealy one each. Once again these names were to feature large during the war.

For Alfred Carter, from Alberta, these were his second and third claims, and later in the year he would fly Triplanes with 10 Naval, to increase his overall score to nine. 'Nick' Carter would achieve seventeen victories by war's end. Harold Kerby, another Canadian, achieved seven victories during March to May and then was posted to Walmer, England, on Home Defence duties. In August 1917, on two separate occasions, he shot down two huge German Gotha G.IV bombers off the English coast.

Lloyd Breadner was also from Canada and during April 1917 he scored on six occasions flying Pups. After the squadron re-equipped with Camels he gained three more in September. He too managed to bring down a Gotha bomber, but over France, on 23 April. It was the first Gotha brought down by a British fighter on the Western Front. Breadner received the DSC. He joined the RCAF after the war, and rose to be Chief of the Air Staff in 1940.

This squadron was well blessed with Canadians, Arthur 'Art' Whealy coming from Toronto. His first victory came on 12 April 1917. Moving to 9 Naval on Triplanes, his score rose to seven by July, at which time he returned to 3 Naval, now flying Camels. He added one more kill before taking a rest, but returned to the squadron in 1918. By early September 1918 he had achieved twenty-seven victories, and been awarded the DSC and Bar and DFC. By that time, of course, 3 Naval RNAS had become 203 Squadron RAF.

During the month the formidable FE.2 crews were achieving good results in bombing and photography, whilst inflicting casualties on those *Jasta* pilots brave enough to engage them. If under serious threat, the FE crews' normal tactic was to form a circle, whereby each pilot and observer could protect the tail of the FE ahead of them. Some of the FE men began to claim heavily in these actions, among them Captain F. R. Cubbon of 20 Squadron, and Captain F. H. Thayre, of the same unit.

Meantime, 56 Squadron had arrived in France with its SE.5 machines, along with Captain Albert Ball, who made his first two claims on the 23rd, his thirty-second and thirty-third victories, one whilst flying a Nieuport. He scored twice more on the 26th, while his thirty-sixth victory came on the 28th. The other flight commanders, Captain Gerald Maxwell and Cyril Crowe, while both new to fighter combat, were starting successful careers, and by the end of 1917 had twenty and nine victories respectively. In fact, 56 would soon become a formidable force to be reckoned with, becoming known unofficially as the squadron of aces. In August it would see the arrival of the man who would become 56's top ace, James McCudden.

As April drew to a close some of the supporting RNAS pilots began to add to their victory totals. E. W. Norton of 6 Naval shared his seventh with a brother pilot on the morning of the 29th. In the afternoon he scored again – twice. Ernest Norton was born in North Wales, but had lived in Scotland. He had received the DSC for destroying a balloon with le Prieur rockets back in October, flying a Nieuport with 1 Naval Wing. Now commanding a flight with 6 Naval he had brought his score to nine. Later in the war he would command 204 Squadron RAF.

The pilots in 8 Naval, or as they became better known 'Naval Eight', were also establishing an enviable record. R. A. Little, from Australia, had flown seaplanes over the North Sea in 1916, then flew Bristol Scouts and bomb raids in Strutters from Dunkirk. Somehow he had time to get married. Joining 8 Naval, he had achieved four victories by early 1917 on Pups, but the squadron was now operating with Sopwith Triplanes. Bob Little had an amazing run of scoring in the Triplane, for by mid-July his score had risen to twenty-eight, to which he added ten more after re-equipping with Camels before that month was out.

Stan Dallas was still scoring, downing his twelfth victory on 30 April, while another new name that was starting to appear was Raymond Collishaw, a Canadian from British Columbia. A former seaman, he had joined the RNAS in January 1916 and flew Strutters on bombing raids with 3 Naval Wing. His aggressive actions resulted in two victories in October, but he then moved to 3 Naval Squadron and Sopwith Pups. Two more victories came and then the Triplanes arrived and, like Bob Little, his score rose rapidly. The last day of April 1917 saw him achieve his sixth victory, having moved to 10 Naval. As a flight commander, he always led from the front and by the end of the year his score was almost forty.

* *

Meanwhile, on the French front the offensive had not gone well after a reasonable start and had stalled by mid-April. The French armies had suffered massive casualties, and this, on top of the losses during the earlier Verdun battles, eventually led to mutiny among the troops.

Nevertheless, French fighter pilots had seen some action in April. Paul Tarascon's *N62* had now become *Spa62* having re-equipped with Spads. He scored twice in April to bring his total to ten. Armand Pinsard of *N78* brought his score to ten by

21 April, having added nine to his one 1916 victory. He would survive the war with twenty-seven claims, and the *Legion d'Honneur.* Raoul Lufbery of *N124* downed his ninth on 14 April. Deullin and Dorme continued unabated, the former scoring number fourteen on 22 April, Dorme his twenty-first on the 29th. Another rising star, Georges Felix Madon, with *N38*, gained his ninth on 24 April. He would survive the war with forty-one victories.

The Arras Offensive dragged on until 16 May without much gain. The British suffered over 158,000 casualties, the Germans 130,000. As far as the British flying services were concerned, April became the bloodiest month thus far, with 211 airmen killed or missing, 108 taken prisoner, plus others lost in flying accidents. Some 245 aeroplanes of all types were lost. The French lost in the region of sixty-three airmen killed, at least eleven captured. Around fifty-five aircraft were lost. The Somme battles in 1916 cost the RFC and RNAS 499 airmen, but that was over nearly five months, between 1 July and 19 November.

An FE.2 of 20 Squadron. Although a large aircraft it was more than capable of surviving in combat with the nimble Albatros and Halberstadt Scouts the *Jastas* flew. This picture demonstrates the lattice tail, enabling the engine to be mounted behind the gondola. The Germans called them *Gitterrümpfe*. This sometimes led to confusion by ground observers, when often they did not differentiate between FE.2s, DH.2s or FE.8s.

A line-up of Albatros D.III and D.V Scouts of *Jasta 5* at Boistrincourt with their cross *pattée* markings. The visual difference between the two types is that the D.III had square rudders and a slab-sided fuselage, whereas the D.V had a rounded rudder and a more rounded fuselage. Aircraft carried personal markings of the pilot for easy identification in the air. For instance, on the third aircraft is an *Eidelweiss*, used by Paul Bäumer, while the one farther along with the black-and-white square was flown by Otto Könnecke.

A group of aces of *Jasta 5* with their overall scores noted in brackets. L to R: -?-, Fritz Rumey (45), Paul Bäumer (43), Josef Mai (30) and Otto Könnecke (35).

Captain Albert Ball DSO MC seated in his 56 Squadron SE.5 at London Colney shortly before the squadron moved to France on 7 April 1917. Note the Lewis gun on the top wing, fixed to fire over the arc of the propeller. The SE.5 also had a single Vickers gun in front of the pilot, firing through the propeller. The previous year, Ball had become proficient in sneaking up on German two-seaters from below in Nieuport Scouts and, by pulling down the wing Lewis gun, was able to surprise his opponents by firing upwards into their machines. As senior flight commander with 56, his victory score was already over thirty. In one month he raised this score to forty-four but was killed in early May.

A good view of how the top-wing Lewis gun could be pulled down in order to fire upwards or to change the ammunition drum. In this particular picture the drum is not in place.

Another view of the wing gun on the SE.5, along with the Bowden cable which enabled the pilot to engage the trigger. This gun too is minus its ammunition drum, no doubt because it is being reloaded. The Aldis gun-sight is also a prominent feature in this picture. The smiling pilot is Lt H. G. Reeves of 1 Squadron who achieved twelve victories before being killed in a flying accident on 24 January 1918.

The Sopwith Pup was a mainstay of RNAS and RFC fighter squadrons by early 1917. A nice aeroplane to fly, a good pilot could take on the new German Albatros machines. This particular Pup is unusual in having a wing-mounted Lewis gun as, generally, they only carried a single fuselage-mounted Vickers gun. This machine was flown by Lt W. A. Pritt of 66 Squadron in the summer of 1917, which brought him the award of the Military Cross.

Lt W. A. Pritt MC of 66 Squadron who claimed six victories, mainly in B1732 (pictured). He came from Leamington Spa and, although nineteen years of age, he looked much younger, almost under-age. Sadly, Pritt was killed in a car crash in January 1928.

A Bristol F.2b fighter. Despite its poor start with 48 Squadron, once handled in an aggressive rather than passive way a good pilot and observer team was able to outfight most opposition. This machine flew with 22 Squadron.

The Sopwith Triplane. This is N500, the prototype machine, which was flown and tested by Captain R. S. Dallas. This un-camouflaged machine is seen after its arrival at St Pol in June 1916. Triplanes served in several **RNAS** squadrons during 1917, perhaps most famously with 10 Naval.

The RFC continued to fly the French Nieuport Scouts in 1917. This No. 1 Squadron machine, with Captain W. W. Rogers in the cockpit, clearly shows the wing-mounted Lewis gun and the cable that allowed the pilot to fire it. Also clearly seen is the telescopic sight giving the pilot every chance of scoring against an opponent ahead of him. Wendell Rogers, a Canadian, received the MC for his air fighting, ending 1917 with nine victories. Included in his score was a Gotha bomber which he shot down in daylight on 12 December.

This French Nieuport XVII of *Escadrille N48*, came down intact behind the German lines and has had its roundels and tail stripes overpainted with the Iron Cross.

Another French Nieuport Scout in German hands. This machine of *Escadrille N506* (No. 2405), was flown by *Brigadier* (equivalent to corporal) Lambert, was brought down and captured by *OfStv* Hüttner of *Jasta 14* on 11 February 1917, his first of three victories.

John Joseph Malone, from Canada, who flew with 3 Naval Squadron in early 1917 and gained ten victories and the DSO before falling to Paul Billick of *Jasta 12* on 30 April. The aircraft is a Sopwith Pup, Malone having also christened his mount as 'The Pup'.

Otto Bernert standing by his *Jasta 4* Albatros Scout. On the eve of the opening of the Battle of Arras he downed a BF.2a of 48 Squadron for his sixteenth victory. Moments later he shot down a Nieuport. Awarded the *Pour le Mérite* on 23 April, he celebrated on the 24th by shooting down five British machines in twenty minutes – a record. By May his score stood at twenty-six. He died on 18 October 1918, a victim of the influenza pandemic.

The *Jastas* were mostly equipped with Albatros D.II and D.III fighters. Each of these D.IIs of *Jasta 16b* (the 'b' denoting a Bavarian unit) have a personal marking for identification in the air. The one marked with a diamond was flown by Ludwig Hanstein who achieved sixteen victories before his death in March 1918. Although Prussian by birth, he served in Bavarian *Jastas*, falling when commanding *Jasta 35b*.

Lloyd Breadner of 3 Naval Squadron by his Sopwith Pup (N6181), named 'Happy'. A Canadian from Carlton Place, Ontario, his first victory was a Halberstadt D.II scout on 6 April 1917. He added five more during the momentous month of April and brought his score to ten by September. Post-war he joined the Royal Canadian Air Force, rising to the rank of air chief marshal as its Chief of Staff. He died in 1953, aged 59.

Sub-Lt J. S. T. Fall, of 3 Naval Squadron, standing beside Lloyd Breadner's Sopwith Pup, N6181. Joe Fall, from Hillbank, British Columbia, would end 1917 with thirty-six victories, the DSC and two Bars. He scored his first seven victories during the Battle of Arras. He remained in the RAF until after the Second World War, with the rank of group captain and died in 1988, aged 93.

Heinrich Gontermann of *Jasta 5* was killed during a test flight in a Fokker Triplane in October 1917. By then he was leader of *Jasta 15*. With a total of thirty-nine victories his prowess had brought him the *Pour le Mérite*, and included in his score were no fewer than eighteen observation balloons. He is standing by his Albatros Scout, which the RFC called 'V-Strutters', for obvious reasons.

Kurt Schneider of *Jasta 5*, gained fifteen victories, ten during April 1917. On 23 April he scored three victories, two of which collided whilst being attacked by him. Badly wounded on 5 June he succumbed to blood poisoning on 14 July. He was downed by the FE.2b crewed by Captain C. M. Clement of 22 Squadron, and his observer, 2/Lt L. G. Davies.

Captain C. M. Clement, a Canadian, accounted for fourteen victories by August 1917. Either his seventh or eighth was Kurt Schneider of *Jasta 5*. Carleton Clement's FE.2b was shot down by anti-aircraft fire on 19 August, and he did not survive.

Hubert Broad was another pilot with 3 Naval in 1917. He later flew with 46 Squadron RAF and, after the war, became chief test pilot for the de Havilland Aircraft Company.

Flight Commander Francis Dominick Casey was another successful pilot with 3 Naval Squadron. From Clonmel, Ireland, he scored nine victories between March and May 1917 and was awarded the DSC. On 11 August, while testing one of the new Sopwith Camels, he got into a spin and crashed before he could recover. He was a week past his 27th birthday. In this picture he is standing in front of one of the squadron's new Camels, so it was taken very shortly before his death. Any number of Pup pilots were killed in the Camel, whose large rotary engine tended to pull the aircraft over into a spin if not handled carefully. Compared to the more docile Pup, the Camel had to be flown through all manoeuvres.

Two more stalwarts with 3 Naval were A. T. Whealy and J. J. Malone. Art Whealy, from Toronto, began his scoring run during the Arras battles and had scored eight victories by September. Having moved to 9 Naval in early May, he returned to 3 Naval shortly afterwards. He remained with 3 Naval, which became 203 Squadron RAF, for the next year, bringing his score to twenty-seven, for which he received the DSC and Bar and the DFC. He died in 1945 in Quebec. John Malone, born in America of Canadian parents, achieved ten victories, six of them during the Arras offensive, for which he received the DSO.

From Calgary, Canada, Captain H. S. Kerby (left) pictured when commanding No. 4 Flying School Friston in 1918. During the early part of 1917 he flew with 3 Naval Squadron, scoring six victories, mostly during April. He was then posted to the Royal Naval Air Station at Walmer and, flying Home Defence sorties, shot down two giant Gotha bombers off the south-east coast of England. He received the DSC and later the AFC for his training abilities. He rose to wing commander in the RAF and pre-Second World War was air attaché in both Peking and Shanghai, during what must have been a very interesting time. Group Captain Harold Kerby died in 1963. On the right Lt E. D. G. Galley who had served in 56 Squadron.

Herbert Travers, from London, England, transferred to the RNAS after serving as a machine gunner in the Honourable Artillery Company, where he had been wounded. He gained five victories with 3 Naval Squadron in March and April 1917, receiving the DSC. 'Tiny' Travers continued to fly post-war, being a test pilot in Greece for the Blackburn Aeroplane Company, and later a flying instructor in England. He joined the RAF again in 1939 for war service and died in 1958.

Lt Paul Billik, who shot down John Malone on 30 April, 1917. He later flew with *Jasta 7* before commanding *Jasta 52.* After scoring thirty-one victories he was brought down inside Allied lines in August 1918, probably by Lt M. C. Kinney of 3 Squadron RAF. By a strange coincidence it was Kinney's first victory, just as Malone's had been Billik's first. Being taken prisoner, and although already nominated for the *Pour le Mérite*, his capture precluded him receiving this award. The swastika was a good luck symbol long before it had Nazi connotations.

Observers could also become aces, and one such was Captain Francis Cubbon of 20 Squadron. Born in London, he was living in Poona, India, when the war began and joined the army. Moving to the RFC in late 1916 he served with this FE.2b Squadron, flying mostly with Captain F. H. Thayre. This very successful team accounted for a large number of German aircraft shot down, Cubbon's contribution being twenty-one, for which he received the MC and Bar. Both were killed on 9 June 1917 by a direct hit from an anti-aircraft shell.

Captain F. J. H. Thayre, also London born, saw service with the Honourable Artillery Company when war began. Transferring to the RFC he first flew with a Corps squadron before moving to 20 Squadron, where his usual observer was F. R. Cubbon. His total score by the time of his and Cubbon's death, was twenty, for which he too received the MC and Bar. It was generally accepted that a two-seater pilot was credited with aircraft shot down by him and his observer, whereas the observer usually only had credit for those he shot down with his rear gun(s).

Armand Pinsard ended the war with twenty-seven victories, seven being achieved during April 1917. He too was somewhat older than many pilots, being almost 30 whilst serving with N78 and Spa23. With this latter unit he shot down nine balloons in 1918. He remained in the French Air Force after the war, and at the start of the Second World War served at the front, losing a leg on 6 June 1940 during a bombing raid. He died in 1953.

Robert Little came from Australia and served with the RNAS, initially on flying boats. Once transferred to fighting scouts, he flew Pups and Triplanes with 8 Naval and, between November 1916 and July 1917, shot down thirty-eight enemy aeroplanes. He was awarded the DSO and Bar and DSC and Bar. During a period of ill-health in 1916 he married and had a son. In 1918 he joined Ray Collishaw's 203 Squadron, raising his score to forty-seven, but, trying to down a Gotha bomber at night in May 1918, he was wounded by return fire, crashed and bled to death before he was found. He was 22 years old.

Sopwith Triplane of 8 Naval Squadron. Named 'Hilda' (N5454), it was the usual machine flown by Reggie Soar DSC who achieved twelve victories during his war service.

Georges Madon was born in Tunisia and learned to fly in 1911. He gained nineteen victories between September 1916 and December 1917. Before flying scouts, he was flying a two-seater and became lost, force landing in Switzerland, where he was interned. He managed to escape and, once returned, was immediately given sixty days' confinement for his trouble. Once he began flying fighters with *N38*, his air fighting skills became apparent, and by September 1918 his victories totalled forty-one. Also credited with a large number of probables, he was killed in a flying accident in 1924.

Two successful French pilots serving with *Escadrille N3*, by a Nieuport Scout, marked with the unit's red stork emblem. On the left is Albert Deullin who had scored ten victories by the end of 1916, adding a further nine in 1917, and one more in 1918. He died in a test flight in 1923. On the right is Paul Tarascon, who flew with *N62* in 1916 and *Spa62* after equipping with Spads in 1917. He brought his score to ten during April 1917. Older than most, he was thirty-four in 1916. Although he lost his right foot in a crash whilst training, this did not stop his desire to fly. Overall he shot down twelve enemy machines during the war. In the Second World War he served with the French Resistance. He died in 1977, aged 94.

Chapter 3
New Aeroplanes, New Tactics

The Battle of Arras that had seen Bloody April dragged on until mid-May 1917 and, as usual, there was little to show for the huge casualties suffered by both sides. The German *Jasta* pilots had become massively enthusiastic about their Albatros and Halberstadt biplane fighters, and forming fighters into independent units as Boelcke had envisioned had been a success.

Apart from a few *Jastas*, such as *Jastas* 2, 5, 10 and 11, most other *Jastas* seemed to progress with a tactic which appeared to work. As soon as one pilot proved himself capable in downing Allied aeroplanes, he began to lead attacks on enemy formations whilst being supported and defended by the other pilots. This is borne out by examining *Jasta* records where one sees perhaps one or two pilots with rising scores while the others occasionally managed to down just a handful of opponents as they were too busy defending the men leading and scoring. For example, *Jasta* 3's leading light was *Vizefeldwebel* Carl Menckhoff, from Westphalia, who at thirty years of age, was older than most, and had been in the German army since 1903. Wounded in the infantry, he had joined the Air Service and came to *Jasta* 3 in early 1917, downing his first two RFC machines on 5 and 6 April, and his third on the 30th. By the end of the year he had eighteen victories, and before he was shot down and captured on 25 July 1918, the total was thirty-nine, and he had received the Blue Max. As a matter of interest he later escaped into Switzerland, where he eventually settled, becoming a businessman until his death in 1948.

These *Jastas* did not always have successful combat pilots as leaders. *Jasta* 6 was another unit that had its *experten*, with *Leutnant* Hans Adam, who arrived from *Jasta* 34b in mid-April, and amassed a total of twenty-one before being killed in November. By that time he had been commissioned and, being a Bavarian, had received the Knight's Cross of the Military Max-Joseph Order, thus becoming Ritter von Adam. He was made *Staffelführer* in August but was shot down by Lieutenant K. B. Montgomery of 45 Squadron, flying a Camel.

Adam had succeeded Oberleutnant Eduard Ritter von Dostler, another Bavarian, as CO. He too had been with *Jasta 34b* prior to *Jasta 6* and came with a score of eight in June 1917. He died while attacking an RE.8 two-seater on 21 August, with his score at twenty-six. Unlike Adam, he received the *Pour le Mérite* but was only made Ritter von Dostler posthumously.

Leaders of *Jasta 2*, like Bernert or Erwin Böhme, were well to the fore in scoring in 1917 while Kurt Schneider and Werner Voss also led *Jasta 5* from the front. Voss had achieved twenty-eight kills by May 1917 with *Jasta 2* before being given command of *Jasta 5*. He had added a further five kills by the time he was given command of *Jasta 10* in August, and he had not yet finished. During Bloody April, *Jasta 11* had four of its pilots leading the tally board, Kurt Wolff with twenty-three, Manfred von Richthofen with twenty-two, Karl Schäfer with twenty-one and Lothar von Richthofen with fifteen. Sebastian Fester was eighth on the list with ten. Close behind them was Karl Allmenröder, also *Jasta 11* and known as 'Karlchen'. From the Rhineland and the son of a pastor, his four victories in April brought his score to nine. By the second half of June this had risen to thirty, along with the award of the *Pour le Mérite*. He fell to ground fire on 27 June, coming down in no man's land but, when darkness fell, soldiers went out and retrieved his body.

Jasta 11 headed the April leader board with eighty-nine victories; *Jasta 5* had downed thirty-two, while *Jasta 12* came third with twenty-three. *Oberleutnant*. Adolf von Tutschek led *Jasta 12* from 28 April, arriving with a modest three victories with *Jasta Boelcke*. At the end of the year this had risen to twenty-three, by which time he had received the *Pour le Mérite*. He had also survived a shoot down by two pilots of 8 Naval Squadron, C. D. Booker and W. L. Jordan.

The loss of Albert Ball on 7 May 1917 came as a bitter blow to the RFC. Between 56 Squadron's arrival in France on 23 April until his death on 7 May, 20-year old Ball had brought his score to forty-four, eleven with the SE.5, two with a Nieuport. To be clear, this was not forty-four German aircraft destroyed; the credit system broke this score down to twenty-seven and one shared destroyed, one balloon destroyed and six 'out of control', with a further nine 'forced to land'. In the early days of the war these 'forced to land' claims were credited, even though it could easily be a

German pilot landing unhurt and his aircraft undamaged; but just as easily it could mean a mortally wounded pilot. By 1917 they became no more than a moral victory. German pilots could land easily, knowing they were down on their own side, while an Allied pilot coming down in similar fashion would be taken prisoner.

Initially there was some controversy on how Ball had been lost. Having found his dead body and crashed aircraft, but with no obvious victor, the Germans naturally decided it would be good for morale to produce a victor. The nearest was a claim that same evening by Lothar von Richthofen, although the fact that he had claimed a Sopwith Triplane didn't seem to matter. It has since been determined that Ball most probably became disorientated in cloud and, coming out at low level at a peculiar angle, did not have time to recover before he hit the ground. His prowess, especially at such a young age, had already brought him the DSO and two Bars, an MC and, now, a posthumous Victoria Cross.

* *

Although RNAS fighter squadrons had been supporting the RFC on the Western Front, it still maintained a huge presence along the French coast and North Sea. One fighter unit was the St Pol Seaplane Defence Flight near Dunkirk, equipped with Sopwith Pups and 1½ Strutters, tasked to help protect the Navy's seaplanes. Two prominent pilots were Ronald Graham and Leonard Slatter. Both would become minor aces, and Graham would command the unit once it was enlarged to become 13 Naval Squadron. He also made his first two claims, flying a Sopwith Baby and a Pup.

Leonard Slatter came from Durban, South Africa, and served as a despatch rider with an armoured car unit before joining the RNAS. He did a lot of flying in seaplanes as an observer before training to be a pilot. In the summer and autumn of 1917, with the Defence Flight, he shot down three German seaplanes and an Albatros Scout, one in a Pup, then three in a Camel. Both men received the DSC.

History tends to overlook the almost private air war over, around and along the North Sea coast, fought between the RNAS units around the Dunkirk area, and the fighter pilots of the German *Marine-Feldjagdstaffeln*. The RNAS were continually supporting actions which would hinder sea and, especially, submarine activity from ports such as Ostende, Vlissingen (Flushing) and Zeebrugge. Their bombers were raiding these ports and the Naval fighter squadrons flew in support. The Germans flew both sea and land planes. Gotthard Sachsenberg, from Dessau, began flying as a naval observer before learning to fly, and flew Eindeckers in 1916. Given command of *MFJ I* in February 1917, his first combat victories came on 1 May, downing a Farman and a Strutter of the Belgian Air Service.

The Belgian forces, now in control of only about a third of their tiny country following the early German advance, continued to hold the line that stretched across their land. They could not promise to be offensive, but their King said that the Allies could count on them defending their end of the line, and they did. Their comparatively small air force was always ready for action.

By the end of 1917 Sachsenberg had eight victories and would end the war with thirty-one. The other famous naval flyer was Friedrich Christiansen. A former seaman, he had become a pilot before the war began and, at age 35, was stationed at Zeebrugge in 1915, flying Brandenburg W.12 seaplanes, operating over the North Sea against UK seaplanes. When air actions developed it could be against the RNAS, Belgians or French Navy aircraft. He eventually commanded the Naval Air Station at Zeebrugge. At the end of 1917 he had achieved at least three victories, including the British airship C.27, but in 1918 he and his men were engaging the large British seaplanes such as the Curtiss H and Felixstowe F.2A, as well as Short 184s.

Another successful pilot with *MFJ I* was Theodor Osterkamp, who joined the Naval Flying Corps as an observer for the first two years of the war, flying along the North Sea coast. In early 1917 he became a pilot, going to *MFJ I* and shooting down a Belgian Nieuport on 30 April. By the late summer his score was six and included a Triplane, an SE.5, a Spad and a couple of Sopwith types. In 1918 he commanded *MFJ III* and ended the war with thirty-two kills. In 1935 he joined Hitler's new *Luftwaffe,* and in the early part of the Second World War commanded a fighter squadron, shooting down six Allied aircraft despite his 48 years.

Meanwhile, the Camels were arriving in numbers during 1917, the first going to 4 Naval in May, the initial encounters taking place early the following month; A. M. Shook made the first claims. A month later Shook shot down a Gotha that was heading for England. As his squadron was based at Bray Dunes, on the North Sea coast, it was strategically placed to intercept such raiders. Whether it was lost remains a question mark, but it was going down with one engine smoking badly.

No. 6 Naval was next to be re-equipped, losing its Nieuports, and gradually Camels began to be sent to 3, 8 and 9 Squadrons. No. 10 Naval, too, lost its Triplanes in favour of Camels but not before it made history with its Black Flight, under Ray Collishaw. Collishaw had moved from 3 to 10 Naval in April and by the time Camels began arriving in July he had achieved around forty victories. He commanded C Flight, whose identity was marked by it having black engine cowlings and wheel covers. The pilots each named their machines with the word 'black' in the title: *Black Maria*, *Black Death*, *Black Prince*, etc.

Colly's pilots all achieved much success in the air. E. V. Reid DSC had nineteen victories before being shot down by AA fire; J. E Sharman, eight victories, also died from AA fire. J. A. Page and John Sharman were both shot down in an air battle with *Jastas 11* and *28*, although there is some discussion about these two possibly colliding in the scrap, but the Germans claimed them anyway. They are buried next to each other in Pont-du-Hem Cemetery. John Page had seven victory claims and W. M. Alexander ended his war with over twenty victories, half of them on the Triplane, with 10 Naval and later when it became 210 Squadron RAF.

By the end of April, the top four German aces were von Richthofen fifty-two, Kurt Wolff twenty-seven, Werner Voss twenty-four and Fritz Bernert twenty-four. The Baron was back in Germany on leave, but his last day at the front was on the 29th, his score being forty-eight. Determined to try to get his fiftieth before he left, he used his day well. At around midday a Spad VII of 19 Squadron made it forty-nine. In the afternoon came the fiftieth, an FE.2b of 18 Squadron. However, he had time in the early evening for another patrol, downing two more British machines, a BE.2c and a Naval Triplane.

＊ ＊

By the middle of 1917 the two main RFC fighters at the front were the SE.5A and Sopwith Camel, with the RNAS operating their Triplanes. One up-and-coming SE.5A pilot was Captain J. T. B. McCudden of 56 Squadron. A former boy-soldier, he had transferred to the RFC as a mechanic in 1913 and went to France as such, with 3

Squadron, occasionally flying as an observer. This led to him being selected for pilot training, having by this time been rewarded with the Military Medal and French *Croix de Guerre*.

Back in France as a sergeant-pilot, he flew DH.2 fighters with 29 Squadron from late 1916 to summer 1917, being commissioned and adding a Military Cross to his decorations. Given command of a flight in 56 Squadron, his already vast experience made him an ideal patrol leader, in what was becoming a veritable squadron of aces. His flying skill also allowed him to fly lone patrols in pursuit of German two-seat reconnaissance patrols although, in general, flying alone over the lines was being frowned upon in favour of patrols of flight strength. Nevertheless, of his thirty-seven victories as 1917 came to an end, no fewer than fourteen two-seaters had not only been shot down, but had fallen within the Allied lines, for which more decorations were bestowed upon him.

Captain R. T. C. Hoidge, from Toronto, Canada, was another huge scorer with 56 Squadron. His first three claims came while the Arras battle was still raging and by the end of 1917 his score stood at twenty-seven. G. J. C. Maxwell, a Scot, and nephew of Lord Lovat was next. He too came out with 56 in April, gaining his first victory before the month was out. He ended the year with twenty victories, continuing to score in 1918. R. A. Maybery, from Wales, had served with the 21st Lancers before moving to the RFC while in Egypt. Flying as an observer he then undertook flight training and, having returned to England, joined 56 in June 1917. The following month he downed six German aircraft in quick succession. On 19 December it was reported that he had shot down his twenty-first enemy, only to be shot down himself afterwards by AA fire and killed. One discovers that Maybery, like so many other First World War fighter pilots, seemed to arrive in France, rise and soar like a meteor, only to die at the height of his fame.

However, there were the lucky ones, such as G. H. Bowman in 56. He had been in 29 Squadron at the same time as McCudden where, despite flying a DH.2, he managed to flame two balloons. After a rest, he was sent to 56 in May 1917 and in short order began cutting a swathe through the German Air Service. By the end of the year his two victories had risen to twenty-two. In 1918 'Beery' as he was called, was sent to command 41 Squadron and although squadron commanders were not encouraged to fly combat he did, and brought his score to thirty-two. Remaining in the RAF after the war, he lived until 1970.

Before leaving 56 Squadron's successful airmen I should mention L. M. Barlow, from London. As soon as he became 18 years of age in 1916 he joined the RFC to train as a pilot. Having done so, he was sent to 56 Squadron, going to France with it in April 1917. He began scoring almost at once and by the first day of October had brought his score to twenty, three of them falling in one fight on 25 September. This was probably the fight with *Jasta 10*, who had two pilots killed. Leonard Barlow survived his time with 56 and, returning to England, having been awarded the MC and two Bars, spent time at Martlesham Heath as a test pilot. On 5 February 1918 he was flying one of the new Sopwith Dolphin machines, but it burst into flames at 150 feet and he fell to his death.

As mentioned earlier the SE.5 had a Vickers gun and a wing-mounted Lewis, which were supposed to be fired independently. Known as 'the gadget king', Barlow had arranged for both guns to fire at once from the same trigger. This, supposedly, followed his idea that, if on target, give it the lot!

The Germans, with their individual *Jastas* being smaller than British or French squadrons, were more inclined to fly in groups of *Jastas* whenever possible. In June 1917, however, the first *Jagdgeschwader* was formed, under the leadership of Manfred von Richthofen, which grouped four *Jastas* together, Nos. 4, 6, 10 and 11. This provided a single command of thirty or forty aircraft able to operate in force, although it rarely operated with more than two *Jastas* on one mission. The overall idea was not new. There were also *Jagdgruppen* being formed, although unlike *JGI*, which was a permanent arrangement, these *Jagdgruppen* (*JGr*) were non-permanent and formed usually for short periods in order to support a specific operation.

The first of these was a Sixth Army *Jagdgruppe*, formed from 30 April until 1 June. It comprised of *Jastas 3, 4, 11* and *33* and would be commanded by von Richthofen upon his return to France, which, with some adjustments, then developed into *JGI*. As 1917 progressed more *Jagdgruppen* were formed, and either had the name of an area where it was operating, or was named after the leader, e.g. *Jagdgruppe* 'Dixmuiden', with *Jastas 7, 29, 33* and *35b*, operated between 20 October and 28 November 1917 in northern Belgium, commanded by *Oberleutnant* Harald Auffahrt. *Jagdgruppe* 'Tutschek', with *Jastas 12, 30* and *37*, only existed for one week, 4-11 August 1917, and was led by *Oberleutnant* Adolf von Tutschek. No doubt its short life was due to von Tutschek, after gaining twenty-three victories, being, as mentioned earlier, shot down and wounded on the 11th by Naval 8.

Charles Booker came from Kent but had lived in Australia until 1911 when his parents returned to England. Joining the RNAS straight from school in 1915 he ended up with 8 Naval in late 1916 although he didn't claim his first victory until January 1917, flying a Pup. Once the squadron re-equipped with Triplanes, his skill quickly developed and by September, during which he scored his first Camel victory, his score had risen to twenty-three.

From these small formation developments came larger *Jagdgruppe* formations at the end of 1917 and into 1918, starting with *JGr Nr.1* in late December, commanded by *Hauptmann* Constantin von Bentheim. These *Jagdgruppen* lasted for most of the war but their individual formations changed constantly and ranged from three to six *Jastas*, but there were always smaller, localised *gruppen* throughout 1918.

Reading through British First World War combat reports, one invariably reads about small flights of SE.5s or Camels engaging in fights with twenty to thirty hostile aircraft, as two or three *Jastas* flew together. However, it could be a problem for the *Jastas* to form up as, generally, they operated from different airfields. Without radio and with cloudy weather prevailing, it was difficult for a leader to get everyone together. Even then it was almost impossible for one man to control large numbers of fighters. The main benefit of these *gruppen* was one of administration but, if the weather was good, German fighter pilots could outnumber the Allied opposition, and they still had the benefit of operating over their side of the lines should a pilot be forced to get down quickly and safely.

Chivalry has often been spoken about with these First World War 'Knights of the Air' but in reality it didn't always happen. Losing close friends, who perhaps had been seen to go down in flames, hardened attitudes to the enemy. Going down and landing in the early years of the war could be fairly safe but during 1917 a German pilot doing this in the hope of flying and fighting another day was often in danger from his recent opponent shooting him up on the ground. Balloon observers too generally took to their parachutes when danger loomed, but sometimes a British or French pilot would do their utmost to shoot up the man as he drifted earthwards. I remember reading one report where the pilot admitted soulfully that he had missed hitting a parachutist. Occasionally one reads of a German, having seemingly bested his British opponent, fly close and wave to him, before winging over and flying back to his base. It would be nice to think he was letting him go, but more than likely the German was out of ammunition and had little choice. As the war progressed brotherly love in an air fight lessened more and more.

The Third Battle of Ypres (commonly known as Passchendaele) was fought between 31 July and November 1917 and saw the British, with some French support, succeed in pushing the lines back two to three miles. But, as the winter weather came along, the area around the town of Passchendaele became a quagmire of death and destruction.

The RFC gave massive support to the armies on the ground and cooperation between aircraft directing artillery fire and the guns was down to a fine art by this stage. More and more aircraft were also employed in ground strafing and bombing, and despite the German *Jasta* pilots claiming many kills over Corps and bombing squadrons, there never seemed to be a reduction in the Allied air efforts.

Baron von Richthofen was wounded in a fight with FE.2s on 6 July as the British armies prepared for the battle. While he recovered from his injury, *JGI* was commanded by *Oberleutnant* Kurt von Döring. Döring had been with a dragoon regiment pre-war, but transferred to aviation in 1913 and, following the declaration of war, went to a two-seater *abteilung*, but by April 1917 he had moved to fighters with *Jasta 4*, claiming his first victory on the 14th. Richthofen obviously saw much more in him than a mere fighter pilot, for when he took command of *JGI* his score was a modest three. He survived the war with eleven victories.

In June, Werner Voss left *Jasta 5*, his score at thirty-four, and a *Pour le Mérite* at his throat. Following a brief stay with *Jasta 29*, von Richthofen wanted him to command *Jasta 10* within his *JGI. JGI* were now flying Fokker Triplanes, Anthony Fokker having been impressed by the Sopwith Triplane and copying the idea. Voss arrived on 30 July and by the end of August had achieved a further four kills (thirty-eight); on 23 September this had risen to forty-eight.

The Fokker Dr.I Triplane has become synonymous with the life of Manfred von Richthofen, it being often overlooked that, of his eventual eighty victories, only the last twenty were scored whilst in a Triplane, the first of these being on 1 September. Anthony Fokker had arranged for the first two Dr.Is to be delivered to *JGI*, the one with serial number 102/17 for the Baron, while 103/17 was for Kurt Wolff, who had commanded *Jasta 11* since the end of June. However, like the Baron, he had been wounded soon after taking over on 11 July. He had returned later to the *Jasta* but, with hand and arm in a sling, was unable to fly.

Voss, therefore, took over 103/17, painting the cowling and rudder bright yellow. He was also due for leave and, similar to the Baron back in April, his own score, at forty-eight, put him in the same position as Manfred, desiring to return to Germany with a score of fifty. On the afternoon of the 23rd, Voss's two soldier brothers arrived so that all three could travel home together, but Voss had time to fly one more patrol, hoping he could down two more British machines.

Taking off alone, something that by this stage of the war was taboo, he headed for the front. Along the way he became aware of a lone Albatros nearby. He then spotted some SE.5s (60 Squadron) and attacked, and in the course of a scrap, damaged two, but not fatally. Voss and the Albatros were then set upon by a patrol of 56 Squadron, led by McCudden, including such aces as Gerald Bowman, Richard Maybery, Reg Hoidge and Arthur Rhys Davids. In the battle that ensued, the Albatros – flown by Carl Menckhoff of *Jasta 3* – was damaged and went down to crash land near Zonnebeke. Voss began to fight the eleven SE.5s and managed to put bullets in every one of the British fighters before he was hit himself. Rhys Davids had scored the lethal burst and saw the Fokker's propeller stop. Whether the engine or a fuel line had been hit, or Voss himself had been wounded, will never be known, but the 19-year old Voss went down and crashed inside Allied lines at Plum Farm, just north-east of Frezenberg at 7.35 pm. He was buried where he fell but the grave was subsequently lost in the battles and shelling that followed.

Rhys Davids was only four days short of his twentieth birthday. He came from south-east London but was living in Surrey when war came. His final school was Eton, where he had been head boy. Joining 56 Squadron he was lucky to survive a tangle with Kurt Wolff on 7 May 1917. However, having survived, he went on to claim twenty-five victories by October before he fell in combat on 27 October, having received the DSO, MC and Bar. His victor was *Leutnant* Karl Gallwitz of *Jasta Boelcke*, the German's fifth victory, of an eventual ten.

Gallwitz, from Baden, was 22-years old and had gone the usual route to become a fighter pilot, via two-seater *abteilung* work. The Germans had a better system than the British. Whereas in the RNAS and RFC once trained, pilots would normally be posted to whatever part of the service needed men, be it reconnaissance, bombing or air fighting. Often arriving at a squadron with very few flying hours in their log-books, it was something of a hit-and-miss affair as to whether they survived long or not. Someone worked out that survival times at the front could be measured in days or weeks, but this is over-simplistic.

The Germans, on the other hand, once trained as pilots, generally started their war flying with two-seater units. In this way they were able to learn how things went at the front and one important part was in learning how to 'see' in the air. It took time for pilots to become aware of their surroundings, and no end of British pilots might return from a patrol having seen nothing, and would be astounded to learn from the others that quite a lot had occurred, and they were lucky not to have been shot down! By the mid-war years the German pilot keen to fly fighters would then go to a Fighter School.

Some German pilots, of course, were happy to remain with two-seater units, having no desire to chase about and get into fights, but the more aggressive men could hardly wait for the chance to transfer. German observers too, who were generally officers, and therefore 'captain' of the two-seater, might get the taste for fighter action and move to become pilots. They might then be posted to single-seaters, having already learnt how things happened at the front. Whatever route they took, they were vastly more experienced and knowledgeable than embryo fighting pilots being sent out from England after a few hours solo flying, and a few days at an air-firing school.

* *

On the French front the constant scorers were, of course, Guynemer, Nungesser and Fonck. Nungesser was constantly being wounded or injured, but continued to come back for more. He spent the first months of 1917 in hospital but finally persuaded his superiors to let him return to the front. They eventually relented and he was attached to *Escadrille VI16* at the end of April. Although this unit was equipped with Voisin aircraft, he was allowed to fly freely with his beloved Nieuport and by August had raised his score to thirty, the last two being Gotha bombers.

Rene Fonck, who became the French ace-of-aces, left his Caudron-equipped *Escadrille C47*, to join *Spa103* in spring 1917. By the end of October he had a score of nineteen victories.

In September, as we have read, the Germans lost the great Werner Voss. Two weeks earlier, on 11 September, France lost Georges Guynemer, his score being fifty-three. He had won every French gallantry award and when asked what further honours could he possibly earn had replied 'the wooden cross'!

Like several of the war's top aces his loss was shrouded in mystery. Out on patrol he simply disappeared in the vicinity of Poelcapelle that morning. Although he was attended to by a German medical officer during a ground battle he succumbed to his injuries, but his burial place, just like that of Voss, was subsequently lost in the fog of battle. The Germans, once they had discovered who had come down, were not sure how it had occurred, but *Leutnant* Kurt Weissmann of *Jasta 3* had put in a claim for a Spad at about the time of Guynemer's loss and in the general area. It was his fifth victory. On the 28th Weissmann himself was killed in combat. There was at one stage a story that Fonck had been the man to down Weissmann, but the Frenchman did not claim a victory on this day. In fact the German fell to a pilot from 56 Squadron. Bowman and Hoidge each claimed an Albatros D.V shot down, and indeed, two of *Jasta 3*'s machines were brought down, one being Weissmann. The other, by strange coincidence, was Carl Menckhoff, the man who had been with Voss in the opening encounter with 56 on the 23rd.

There were very few Belgian aces in the First World War, but two who were prominent in 1917 were Edmund Thieffry and Andre Demeulemeester. Thieffry accounted for ten German aircraft, but he was captured in February 1918, while Demeulemeester, while only receiving credit for six victories, recorded a further nine which were not confirmed. Another Belgian, Willy Coppens, claimed three two-seaters down in 1917, but none were confirmed. A fourth in early 1918 failed to get by 'higher authority'. However, his name would become well known in 1918.

There was also a British pilot whose fame took a while to materialise but, flying Nieuport Scouts with No. 40 Squadron in 1917, he achieved fifteen victories by September 1917. His name was Edward Mannock and we shall hear more about him too in 1918.

Bavarian *Oblt* Eduard Ritter von Dostler did not live to see his name written in such a fashion. Initially he saw service with the army until his brother was shot down and captured in 1916, but by then his bravery had been rewarded with the Iron Cross 1st Class and the Bavarian Military Service Order 4th Class with Swords. Once trained as a pilot he flew two-seaters but in January 1917 became a fighter pilot, with *Jastas 13* and *34b*. By the end of April he could claim six victories and by June eight, at which time he became leader of *Jasta 6*. With a final score of twenty-six, and the *Pour le Mérite,* he was shot down in an encounter with a British RE.8 on 21 August. Posthumously awarded the Bavarian Military Max-Joseph Order, he was made Ritter von Dostler.

Two successful RNAS pilots in 1917 were Alexander Shook and Charles Booker, seen here following the presentation of DSCs. Ontario-born Shook, flying with 4 Naval, had eight victories by the end of 1917 and would survive the war with twelve, plus the DSO and *Croix de Guerre*. Booker, from Kent, flew with Naval 8 in Pups, Triplanes and Camels, scoring twenty-three victories by the end of September. In 1918 he commanded 201 Squadron and before his death on 13 August had downed twenty-nine opponents. He went to the aid of some of his pilots and was shot down by the German ace Ulrich Neckel of *Jasta 12*.

Ulrich Neckel originally served with the artillery on the Eastern Front in 1915 but by late 1916 was beginning his flight training. Back to the East on two-seaters he eventually went to a *Jastaschule*, and then to *Jasta 12* in September 1917. Flying with *Jastas 12, 13, 19* and *6*, he amassed thirty victories by the Armistice, and had received the Blue Max. His twenty-second victory was over Major C. D. Booker on 13 August 1918. After the war Neckel contracted tuberculosis and died in Italy in May 1928.

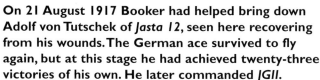

On 21 August 1917 Booker had helped bring down Adolf von Tutschek of *Jasta 12*, seen here recovering from his wounds. The German ace survived to fly again, but at this stage he had achieved twenty-three victories of his own. He later commanded *JGII*.

Karl Allmenröder of *Jasta 11* downed thirty Allied aeroplanes before his death by AA fire on 27 June 1917. Although awarded the *Pour le Mérite* he was not photographed with the Blue Max at his throat, so this photograph is one where this decoration has been painted on after his death.

Allmenröder seated in his Albatros Scout. All *Jasta 11* aircraft had red as part of their unit identification, Allmenröder having his machine's nose and elevators painted white. Upper-wing surfaces were painted light and dark green with some additional reddish brown.

Leonard Slatter flew Pups with the Seaplane Defence Flight on the North Sea coast. He gained four victories by October 1917, by which time he was flying a Camel. Slatter is seated here in his personal Pup, with the name *Mina* painted on the fuselage.

Slatter's Pup, N6203, at St Pol. In addition to the name, there are two white tear-drop markings on the elevators and it has white wheel covers. Slatter rose to the rank of air marshal, commanding 15 Group of Coastal Command in the Second World War, and then becoming C-in-C of Coastal Command. He died in 1961.

Ronnie Graham also had success with the Seaplane Defence Flight in both Pups and Camels. When the Flight became 13 Naval Squadron (then 213), he was given command. He rose to air vice marshal, was appointed **CB CBE** and died in 1967.

The **RNAS** on the French/Belgian coast had an almost private war with the German naval pilots over the North Sea. Friedrich Christiansen, the 38-year old son of a sea captain, became a naval aviat in 1914 and was often engaged in air fights with British flying boats and seaplanes. He was awarded the *Pour le Mérite,* and during the war, flying mostl Brandenburg W.12 seaplanes, had thirteen official victories, or possibly as many as twenty-one. This included the British airship C.27, shot down on 11 December 1917. He died in 1972, also seeing servi in the Second World War.

Ray Collishaw's Black Flight in 10 Naval had some excellent Canadian pilots on strength, including John Sharman and John Page. Sharman, from Manitoba, achieved eight victories and Page, from Ontario, seven. Both were lost on 22 July 1917. Although they were claimed by German pilots there has always been a suspicion that they had collided during combat.

W. M. Alexander, from Toronto, was another 10 Naval pilot. He scored ten victories on Triplanes and Camels in 1917, a total he increased to twenty-two by May 1918. He survived the war with a DSC and died in 1988.

Gerry Nash achieved six victories with 10 Naval. From Stoney Creek, Ontario, all his claims came whilst flying Triplanes, but his success ended abruptly on 26 June, falling to the guns of Karl Allmenröder of *Jasta 11*, the German's twenty-ninth victory. Becoming a prisoner of war, he later served in the RCAF during the Second World War, retiring as a group captain. He died in 1976.

A squadron that was to make a name for itself in the First World War was No. 56. Going to France in April 1917, Albert Ball was one of its flight commanders, but many of his comrades quickly made names for themselves too. The early SE.5s had an elaborate windshield arrangement, seen here, but these were soon discarded once in France. The pilot is R. T. C. Hoidge, of Toronto, whose first victory came on 5 May; by the end of October his total had reached twenty-seven. After home leave he returned to see out the war with No. 1 Squadron, gaining one more victory before the Armistice. He received the MC and Bar and died in New York City in 1963.

Leonard Barlow was a triple MC winner. A Londoner, he joined the RFC as soon as he reached 18 years. He was also a prolific scorer, claiming twenty victories by 1 October. On 25 September he claimed three aircraft shot down, and two of the pilots that went down are believed to have come from *Jasta 10*. He linked his Vickers and Lewis guns to fire at the same time, giving maximum firepower once he was behind the enemy. Sent home for a rest, he flew as a test pilot at Martlesham Heath where his luck ran out on 5 February 1918. He was flying one of the new Sopwith Dolphin machines but, at 150 feet, it began to break up and he crashed in flames. He was still only 19 years old.

As his cap and collar badges show, Welsh born R. A. Maybery had previously been with the 21st Lancers. Joining the RFC in Egypt, he saw service in India with 31 Squadron as an observer, but managed to become a pilot. He arrived on 56 Squadron in June 1917 and quickly established himself as an ace pilot. Awarded the MC and Bar, his claims amounted to twenty-one by December, until his SE.5A was hit by AA fire and he fell to his death on the 19th.

Geoffrey Bowman transferred from the Army to the RFC in March 1916 and, once becoming a pilot, flew DH.2s with 29 Squadron. He claimed two victories with that squadron but was posted to 56 in June 1917. His prowess in air fighting brought him the MC and Bar, and later the DSO and DFC, plus a Belgian *Croix de Guerre*. He ended 1917 with twenty-two victories and by the war's end this had risen to thirty-two. Remaining in the RAF, 'Beery' Bowman became a wing commander in the 1930s but was recalled to duty in the Second World War for a couple of years. He died in 1970.

Another successful pilot with 56 was G. J. H. Maxwell, from Inverness, the nephew of Lord Lovat of Boer War fame. Gerry had seen action at Gallipoli with the Army but moved to the RFC, famously going solo after just twenty-two minutes of dual-control instruction. Posted to 56 Squadron as it prepared for France, he too scored frequently, his score reaching twenty by the end of September. He received the MC before being rested, but returned to 56 in 1918, bringing his score to twenty-six, and collecting the DFC for his efforts. Post-war he worked in the Stock Exchange but also served with the RAuxAF and was then recalled for service in the Second World War. He died in 1959.

When Manfred von Richthofen was wounded on 6 July 1917, Kurt-Bertram von Döring took command of *JGI*. In fact, whenever the Baron was absent he commanded. A former dragoon, he flew two-seaters early in the war and in April 1917 was given command of *Jasta 4*. By the end of the year he had achieved nine victories. In 1918 he took command of *JGr4*, and later commanded two further *Jastas*. Ending the war with eleven victories he continued to serve in the German Air Force, rising to the rank of major general in the Second World War. He died in 1960.

Kurt Wolff, from Pomerania, and a former army cadet was an officer by 1915 but then transferred to aviation. His first war experience was gained flying bombing aircraft during the Verdun and Somme battles, and he then managed a posting to fighters. Joining *Jasta 11* he failed to shoot down any enemy aircraft until after the arrival of Manfred von Richthofen, but from March 1917 suddenly blossomed. With five kills in March to an impressive twenty-two in April he received the *Pour le Mérite*. He was then sent to command *Jasta 29* but returned to lead *Jasta 11* following Richthofen's wounding. His score reached thirty-three on 7 July but he was wounded in the hand four days later. Returning to duty in September he was shot down by a Camel pilot from 10 Naval on 15 September in one of his first flights in the new Fokker Triplane.

Werner Voss with his Triplane shortly before his death in combat, which occurred on 23 September 1917. Fighting a whole unit of SE.5s of 56 Squadron, he managed to put bullets into all of them before being fatally hit by Lt A. P. F. Rhys Davids. He had gained forty-eight victories, mainly with *Jasta 2*, then *Jastas 5* and *11*. He had received the Blue Max and, on the day of his death, was due for home leave, but was no doubt lured by the hope of bringing his score to fifty before leaving for Germany. He was 20 years old.

Arthur Rhys Davids was just four days short of his 20th birthday when he shot down Voss on 23 September 1917. A former Eton scholar he had joined 56 Squadron while it was 'working up' and left with it for France in April 1917. Voss was his nineteenth victory and in the same fight he shot down Carl Menckhoff of *Jasta 3*, who crash-landed. Rhys Davids received the MC and Bar, then the DSO, but fell himself in combat on 27 October, shot down by Karl Gallwitz of *Jasta Boelcke*, his fifth of ten victories.

Karl Gallwitz of *Jasta Boelcke* came through the two-seater route on the Eastern Front in mid-1917, flying the Roland D.III Scout and being credited with two balloon kills. Moving to France, he added eight more victories to his list, including Rhys Davids. Injured in a crash in April 1918 he spent the rest of the war with the *Inspektorate der Flieger*.

Capitaine Alfred Auger flew with *Escadrille N31* in 1916 and commanded *N3* in 1917. Wounded with the infantry early in the war, he became a pilot and was wounded again in 1915 with a two-seater unit. Going to fighters he went to command *N3* in March 1917 and brought his score to seven, with another seven probables. He was killed in combat on 28 July 1917, shot down by Rudolf Francke of *Jasta 8*. Note that his hat still carries the number '31' of his earlier *escadrille* but he has the Stork emblem of *N3* on the jacket.

Rudolf Francke began his war flying as an observer and, after pilot training, joined *Schutzstaffel 17*. In March 1917 he moved to *Jasta 8* where he claimed fifteen victories by the end of the war. Alfred Auger of *N3* should have been his fifth victory, but his claim for a Spad on the French side of the lines went unconfirmed.

Charles Nungessor, seen here with his father. The French ace suffered a number of wounds and injuries during his career in August 1917 had again been injured, but in a car accident. He had achieved thirty victories by this time, but he would return to the front in March 1918. His *escadrille*, now flying Spads, became *Spa65*.

The great Georges Guynemer was lost on 11 September 1917. This pleasing picture of him shows his *Legion d'Honneur, Médaille Militaire and Croix de Guerre* which eventually had twenty-six *Palmes*. He failed to return from patrol and fell near to the front-line battle area. Although it is reported he died in the arms of a German doctor, and was buried near to where he fell, his grave was subsequently lost in the fighting. He had achieved fifty-three victories with at least ten probables. He was 22 years of age.

Although initially it was not known who might have brought down the great Guynemer, the Germans eventually credited him to Kurt Weissmann of Jasta 3, his fifth and final victory. This 24-year old had been an observer before pilot training and had gone through the two-seater route before becoming a pilot. He fell to 56 Squadron on 28 September.

Edmund Thieffry, the Belgian ace, in front of his Nieuport Scout, with the shooting star emblem on its fuselage denoting *5me Escadrille de chasse*. He had ten confirmed and five unconfirmed kills and, although he survived 1917, was shot down and captured on 23 February 1918. Note the Nieuport has an Aldis telescopic gun-sight and one Vickers gun, fixed slightly off centre over the engine cowling. He died in an air crash in 1929, leaving a wife and five children.

Andre Demeulemeester flew with *Escadrille 1ère de chasse*, scoring six official and eight unconfirmed victories in 1917. In 1918 he flew with *9me*, which was equipped with the Hanriot HD.1 Scout. He survived the war with eleven victories and a further seven probables. The aircraft is a British Camel, carrying the thistle marking of *9me*.

Edward Mannock while flying with 40 Squadron in 1917. His story is well known, at one stage being credited with being the highest British air ace of the war. He served with 40 Squadron from April 1917 to 1 January 1918, scoring fifteen victories, for which he received the MC and Bar. In 1918 he became a flight commander with 74 Squadron but died commanding 85 Squadron in July 1918. In 1918 he was awarded the DSO and two Bars and, finally, in 1919, a posthumous VC.

Chapter 4
The Winter of 1917-18

The autumn of 1917 had seen much bloodletting in the skies over France and, although the winter weather would naturally curtail intensive operations, air actions continued.

In November came the Battle of Cambrai in which British tanks featured to a great degree. While the majority of fighter squadrons continued to use Camels and SE.5As, the Bristol F.2b two-seaters were well in evidence and claimed heavily during combats, although one suspects there was a degree of over-claiming. There was another fighter in France now, the Airco DH.5, which was unusual in that it had a back-stagger wing arrangement where the top wing was almost behind the pilot. This was designed to aid the pilot's all-round forward view, important for air fighters, but left the pilot feeling a trifle exposed. It was also believed that should the machine nose-over in a bad landing the pilot would break his neck. It carried a single Vickers gun, fitted to fire through the propeller blades.

Like other new aircraft an example had been tested in France and the first unit to receive them in strength was No. 24, exchanging its old DH.2 pushers, in May 1917. No. 32 Squadron was the next to re-equip. However, trouble with the Constantinesco interrupter gear put both units out of action for a while. By the late summer the DH.5 was found to be a reasonably good machine for ground-strafing and had some success during the Ypres battles. No. 64 Squadron became the third unit to be equipped. The DH.5s were only at the front until late 1917, being finally replaced by the SE.5A. However, one pilot in particular had some success on the type, Captain Arthur Coningham with 32 Squadron. He had just one victory with the DH.2 but during July 1917 accounted for nine enemy machines, which brought him a DSO and MC. Second Lieutenant D. R. P. Walter also gained six victories in July but died following a collision with a balloon cable on the 31st. Lieutenant W. R. G. Pearson scored seven times.

In 24 Squadron a few pilots who would later become aces scored one or two victories with the DH.5, and, in 41, Lieutenant Russell Winnicott gained seven victories, mostly in September. The type also saw some ground attack sorties during Cambrai, but they were soon taken away from the front.

The Germans too had a new fighter in late 1917, the Pfalz D.III, which at first glance looked very similar to the Albatros D.V. A number were distributed amongst the *Jastas*, so they often had a mixture of both types. An improved D.IIIa came along later and remained at the front until the summer, by which time the main fighter being used was the awaited Fokker D.VII.

Several big aces began to fall during early winter 1917. Hans Adam, a Bavarian, was a married man with two children when war came, and aged 28. With the infantry he was wounded early on and then moved to the Air Service. He became an observer, often flying with a future ace, Eduard von Schleich. Becoming a pilot himself, he eventually arrived at *Jasta 34b*, where he gained two victories before moving to *Jasta 6*, a unit he later commanded. On 6 November 1917 his score stood at twenty-one but on the 15th he was shot down and killed in a fight with Camels of 45 Squadron. Adam received a posthumous Bavarian Knight's Cross of the Military Max-Joseph Order and so became Hans Ritter von Adain.

His victor was Lieutenant K. B. Montgomery who had been flying Strutters with 45 Squadron prior to the arrival of the Camel and had already scored four victories. Downing Adam had been victory number ten. It came shortly before the squadron left the Western Front for the Italian Front. He received the MC when his total victories became twelve.

November also saw the loss of Erwin Böhme on the 29th. It had been he who had collided with his friend and mentor Oswald Boelcke just over a year earlier, which led to Boelcke's death. Böhme had continued with *Jasta 2* until he took command of *Jasta 29* in mid-1917, but after one victory, his thirteenth, he returned to *Jasta Boelcke* as its *Staffelführer*. For the rest of the year he continued to add to his score, which reached twenty in October, at which point he would have been nominated for the *Pour le Mérite*. On 29 November he shot down a Camel over Zonnebeke for victory number twenty-four but, as he then attacked an Armstrong-Whitworth FK.8 two-seater of 10 Squadron RFC, the observer got in a telling burst from his Lewis gun and Böhme fell to his death. Had he returned to his office on the airfield he would have found the package containing his Blue Max.

This early winter period was seeing other aces fall. On 2 December, having recently returned from leave – being away from the action often proved fateful – Captain H. G. E. Luchford of 20 Squadron went down. This former Bromley bank clerk had, with his observers, claimed eleven victories in the summer of 1917, before the squadron re-equipped with the BF.2b. By the time he went on leave this score had risen to twenty-four and he had received the MC and Bar. Getting into a fight with *Jasta 36* he was shot down by *Leutnant* Walter von Bülow-Bothkamp and became the German's twenty-eighth and final victory. Bülow received the Blue Max in October and, on 13 December, took command of *Jasta Boelcke*. He did not add to his score before being shot down and killed on 6 January 1918, falling inside Allied lines; he was shot down by Captain W. M. Fry MC of 23 Squadron, flying a Spad, and Lieutenant F. G. Quigley MC in a 70 Squadron Camel.

Willie Fry had a varied war, scoring victories with Nieuports of 60 Squadron during spring, then Spads with 23, while his eleventh and final kill was made flying a Sopwith Dolphin with 79 Squadron on 23 January 1918.

Francis Quigley, from Toronto, had served with the Canadian engineers in the early part of the war before moving to the RFC. Flying with 70 Squadron in the autumn of 1917, he had nine victories by the end of the year and been awarded the MC. The share in von Bülow's death had been his eleventh victory and, towards the end of March 1918, his tally had risen to thirty-three, for which he added a Bar to his MC and then the DSO.

Bülow had a younger brother, Harry, another successful fighter pilot, who had also been with *Jasta 36*, and had scored three times by the end of 1917. He would survive the war with six victories. Another German ace to be shot down in December was Ernst Hess, leader of *Jasta 19*. From Weisbaden, he had learned to fly in 1913 and when war came found himself flying two-seaters in France. He was one of the early Fokker pilots, downing two Allied aircraft in 1916. In mid-1917 he was flying with *Jasta 28w* (the 'w' denoting a Württemburg unit) and by September had amassed a score of fourteen. He then took command of *Jasta 19*, scoring three more times by the end of October, by which time *Jasta 19* was on the French front. On 23 December he was shot down by *Adjutant* de Kergolay of *N96*, the Frenchman's first victory.

One of the participants of the Voss fight back in September had been Richard Maybery of 56 Squadron. On 19 December, having achieved twenty-one victories, his SE.5A was hit by ground fire and he was killed.

Acting commander of *Jasta Boelcke*, following von Bülow's loss, was *Leutnant* Max Müller, a 31-year old Bavarian. It is doubtful whether he would have succeeded in full command because, being Bavarian, it was generally the case that he could not have commanded a Prussian unit, even with the Blue Max at his throat. Added to this, he had been a NCO for a long time and had only been commissioned in August, due mainly to his combat prowess. Aged 31 on 1 January 1918, his score had reached thirty-six, flying with both *Jasta Boelcke* – under the master – and then *Jasta 28w*. With his score standing at twenty-nine he had returned to *Jasta Boelcke* in November. He did not add to his 1917 score by the time he attacked a British RE.8 on 9 January 1918. The crew of Captain G. F. W. Zimmer and Second Lieutenant H. A. Somerville MC (a trenches MC) were assaulted by seven Albatros Scouts although SE.5s of 60 Squadron came to their aid. While thus engaged, Müller went for the two-seater, but Somerville's defensive fire hit the German Albatros which went down in flames.

February 1918 saw several losses of RNAS aces, starting on the 3rd with Flight Commander R. R. Winter of 9 Naval. In 1917 he had flown with 6 Naval where he scored three victories, gaining number four with 9 Naval on 6 December. His fifth came during the action in which he was killed, a Fokker Triplane, shared with another pilot. *Jasta 26* claimed several Camels but only Winter failed to get home.

Naval 8 lost Flight Lieutenant Harold Day DSC on the 5th, and he too had gained a victory – his twelfth – on the day he was killed. Attacking an Albatros Scout, his Camel appeared to break up, although *Leutnant* Günther Schuster of *Jasta 29* put in a claim for him. Schuster's claim was his fourth, to which he would add two more before being seriously wounded in August 1918. After the war he flew with SKADTA Airlines in South America. Day's last three victories were all shared with other pilots.

Perhaps I should mention these shared victories. In the First World War the British usually divided victories between the pilots who had taken part in the destruction, or otherwise, of German aircraft. Therefore, if, say, four pilots had all engaged and fired into a hostile machine that was shot down, each could claim a share. In a pilot's overall score, it would still count as one. To be clear, if a pilot had been credited with three German aircraft destroyed, two 'out of control' and perhaps two shared of either variety, his overall score would be noted as seven.

The Germans did not use the same system, so if two pilots took part in shooting down an Allied aeroplane, and the two pilots – and the *staffel* commander – could not sort it out it would go to arbitration. In this way the victory would eventually be credited only to one pilot. The French also shared victories with each pilot receiving credit if involved. With the arrival of the Americans in 1918, and being attached to the French, they too shared victories but, like the French, did not record probables in a man's overall score.

On 18 February Naval 8 lost another veteran, Flight Commander G. W. Price DSC and Bar. From Dublin, and sporting a 'Captain Kettle beard', he claimed a dozen victories between 5 December and 16 February, four being shared. During a lone low-level strafing mission on the 18th he was attacked and killed by *Leutnant* Theodor Rumpel of *Jasta 23*, his fifth and final victory. Rumpel was badly wounded in March.

The very next day, *Oberleutnant* Hans Klein, leader of *JGI*'s *Jasta 10* was knocked out of the war. When war began he was in the infantry but then transferred to aviation. With *Jasta 4* for the first half of 1917, he achieved sixteen victories by mid-July, before being wounded in a fight with 29 Squadron. Once fit again, he was given command of *Jasta 10* and during October and November brought his score to twenty-two, receiving the Blue Max on 2 December. His final wound, in which he lost his right thumb, ended his war flying. In the Second World War he rose to major general with the *Luftwaffe*.

Over the North Sea on 27 February, a pilot serving with 13 Naval, formerly the Seaplane Defence Flight, Flight Commander M. J. G. Day DSC, was lost. He had achieved five victories since the start of the year but, in a fight with *Seeflug II* seaplanes, he was brought down by return fire. He was seen to crash land and later cling to wreckage but was not rescued.

These early weeks of 1918 were proving costly for both sides on the Western Front, including the aces. On 10 March another high-scoring German pilot fell in combat – *Oberleutnant* Hans-Joachim Buddecke. From Berlin, Buddecke had been a soldier pre-war before going to America to work in his uncle's motor-car plant. He bought a French Nieuport aeroplane and taught himself to fly and, when war came, returned home to join the air service.

In 1915, while attached to a two-seater unit, he flew Fokkers and gained three victories. Life for him changed dramatically upon being posted to the Middle East before the end of the year and, operating over the Gallipoli/Dardanelles sector, shot down five Allied aircraft whilst also claiming seven that were not confirmed. Germany's Turkish allies called him 'The Fighting Hawk'.

He returned to France in 1916, flying with *Jasta 4*, then back to Turkey in 1917, where he brought his overall score to twelve. By this time he had been awarded the *Pour le Mérite* for his actions which, for a fighter pilot, was well below the normal yardstick of twenty victories. Back to France, he became deputy leader of *Jasta 18*. He had taken over from Rudolf Berthold, who was about to command *JGII*. However, on 10 March 1918, Buddecke and Berthold were with a patrol that ran into a Flight of Camels of 3 Naval Squadron, led by Art Whealy DSC.

By this time, however, air fighting on the Western Front had changed since Buddecke had last been active there and, in the fight that developed, Whealy attacked Berthold. Berthold was known as the 'Iron Knight' because he had been wounded on several occasions and it could be argued that he should no longer have been on active service. Buddecke saw the danger and tried to intervene but overshot and appeared in Whealy's gun-sight. Buddecke had saved Berthold but lost his own life in doing so. Although he did not know the occupant of the German fighter, it was Whealy's tenth victory.

* *

By this time the RFC had a new type at the front, the Sopwith Dolphin. It was different from the usual Sopwith designs in that it had an in-line engine rather than a rotary one. Like the DH.5 it had a back-stagger top wing that allowed the pilot's head to protrude through a break in the top wing centre section. It provided a superb view, not obstructed by the top wing at all but, like the DH.5, pilots were wary of the danger of a nose-over in a poor landing.

The first examples, which went to 19 and 23 Squadrons to replace their French Spads, had two hoops either side of the pilot, rather like racing-car crash bars, but these were quickly deemed redundant. The aircraft could have a variety of armament too: all versions carried two Vickers guns in front of the pilot, and had provision for two Lewis guns immediately to his left and right on the top-wing cross member. They could be flexible and as such were more conveniently placed than the wing Lewis gun on the SE.5, but they also tended to move about in the slipstream, so often one and later both guns were removed depending on how the pilot felt. In 87 Squadron, which came to France in April 1918, they experimented with a Lewis gun mounted atop both lower wings, outboard of the propeller arc. These would be fired by a cable from the cockpit but, being out of reach, only carried one non-replaceable drum. It did not become standard.

The Red Baron's brother, Lothar, had a narrow escape from death on 13 March. In a big fight with BF.2bs of 62 Squadron, Camels of 73 Squadron and *JGI*'s Triplanes, Lothar was shot up by the experienced Bristol team of Captains G. F. Hughes and H. Claye. As the Fokker came down behind their Bristol, Claye opened fire with good effect, seeing the top centre section of the Triplane disintegrate. Lothar got his badly-damaged machine down but in the resultant crash-landing suffered a broken jaw. Hughes and Claye thus achieved their sixth victory. Hughes, an Australian, received the MC, then brought his final score to eleven by May. Claye, flying with another pilot, was shot down and captured on 19 May, claimed by fighters and AA fire.

Captain A. H. Orlebar had also got in a shot at the Triplane and put in a claim as his third victory. Orlebar was later head of Britain's Schneider Trophy team. He had quite a varied war, having scored victories with three different squadrons.

No sooner had Lothar von Richthofen been knocked out of the war for several months than the Germans suffered another blow, losing Adolf von Tutschek on the 15th. Leading *JGII*, having returned to duty following his wounding back in August, he had brought his score to twenty-seven on 10 March, but in a fight with 24 Squadron's SE.5As was apparently hit by a burst from Lieutenant H. B. Redler and went down to a forced landing. His men were glad to see him climb out of his Fokker Triplane but, as ground troops reached the spot they found him lying dead by the side of it. There was a graze to his head from which he died, or he had suffered a heart attack. In any event, Harold Redler was credited with his fourth victory of an eventual ten.

Two days later, the 17th, another blow struck. Berliner *Oberleutnant* Hans Bethge had achieved his twentieth victory on 10 March 1918 and might well have been expecting notification of his Blue Max award. He had been another early Fokker Eindecker pilot in 1916 and in spring 1917 had taken command of *Jasta 30*. However, attacking a British two-seater DH.4 in his Pfalz D.III over Passchendaele, its observer once again got in a telling shot, downing the German ace. His nomination for the Blue Max was not progressed, this prestigious award not being awarded posthumously. The DH.4 crew had been Captain A. Roulstone MC and Second Lieutenant W. C. Venmore of 57 Squadron who had both been wounded in this action but got home. Alexander Roulstone and his various observer/gunners had claimed eight German fighters shot down.

This same 17th day of March 80 Camel Squadron lost Captain St C. C Tayler, a 22-year flight commander. Although born in Winchester, he had spent time in Natal, South Africa, but returned to serve with the Royal Sussex Regiment before moving to the RFC. He had scored half a dozen or so victories in the DH.5 with 32 Squadron, receiving the MC, before joining 80. He was shot down by Heinrich Kroll of *Jasta 24*, south of Cambrai. Kroll, the son of a schoolteacher from Kiel, had served in the infantry before flight training and had gone through the two-seater route to fighters. In 1917 he was with *Jasta 9* and then *Jasta 24* from July. Tayler became his twenty-first victory. On 27 July, after becoming commander of *Jasta 24*, Kroll was shot down in flames but miraculously survived. He was probably downed by the American Clive Warman, flying Spads with 23 Squadron, who claimed an 'out of control' victory; perhaps it caught fire later. Warman achieved twelve victories by August and received both the MC and DSO.

On the 18th, James McCudden's younger brother, Anthony, was killed in combat. Flying SE.5s with 84 Squadron, his patrol had got into a fight with a number of German fighters that had been attacking DH.4 bombers. The German aircraft were those of *JGI*. No. 84 were joined by Camels of 54 Squadron and in the fight which developed both sides scored victories. However, 'Jack' McCudden – as he was called – was attacked by Hans Wolff of *Jasta 11*, his first of eleven victories. McCudden had achieved a modest eight victories and been awarded the Military Cross.

The DH.5 fighter was designed to give a pilot the best all-round view, so the top wing was staggered backwards. It saw only limited service in France during the summer of 1917 and was phased out by the end of the year. It carried just a single Vickers gun, and a number were used in England at training schools.

The most successful pilot with the DH.5 was Arthur Coningham with 32 Squadron, who achieved nine of his fourteen victories on the type during July 1917. From Australia, he was known as *Maori* (the nickname arose from his service in Gallipoli with the New Zealanders where he was wounded and discharged as medically unfit. He travelled to the UK at his own expense to volunteer for the RFC) although, over his years in the service, this became *Mary*. He received the DSO and MC, later commanding 92 Squadron in 1918, and was rewarded with the DFC. Remaining in the RAF he rose to air marshal, receiving a knighthood in 1945. He was lost in 1948, the airliner, an Avro Tudor Mk IVB, in which he was flying to Bermuda disappearing en route.

Captain W. R. G. Pearson also had success with the DH.5 with 32 Squadron, claiming seven victories between July and December 1917. He had earlier been with the Army prior to becoming an observer in late 1916. Sadly he was killed in a flying accident at Hooten Park, in June 1918, flying in an Avro 504.

Bavarian *Leutnant* Hans Adam was a married man with children when the war began and twenty-eight years old. He served with the infantry before moving to aviation and, as an observer, flying a number of sorties with future ace Eduard von Schleich as his pilot. Once becoming a fighter pilot, he served with *Jasta 34b* in spring 1917, then *Jasta 6*, which he eventually commanded, within Richthofen's *JGI*. With a score of twenty-one he was killed in action with 45 Squadron on 15 November 1917. He would have been due for the nomination of the *Pour le Mérite* if he had not died. However, he was awarded a posthumous Knight's Cross with Swords of the Bavarian Hohenzollern House Order, becoming, in death, Ritter von Adain.

The death of Hans Adam on 15 November 1917 was attributed to K. B. Montgomery of 45 Squadron, flying a Camel. It was his tenth victory, scored while flying both the Sopwith 1½ Strutter and Camel in 1917. It was his last victory over France, 45 then moving to the Italian Front. He added two more victories to his total before becoming a prisoner in February 1918. He received both the MC and the Italian *Croce de Guerra*.

Erwin Böhme had had to live with the knowledge that his collision with Oswald Boelcke had robbed the German Air Service of its greatest air fighter of the early war years. Yet he himself became a successful fighter ace with *Jasta 2*, which he later commanded. By November his score had reached twenty-three with one more on the 24th, the day he was shot down and killed during an attack on a British two-seater. He had been nominated for the Blue Max, and it was a sad irony that the medal was waiting on his desk on the day he fell. This picture shows the Blue Max painted on the print.

Although born in Lucknow, India, H. G. E Luchford lived in Bromley, Kent, when his family returned to England. Initially with the Army, being commissioned with the ASC in September 1914, he later was with the Indian Cavalry Division. Moving to aviation he flew FE.2s with 20 Squadron in 1917, and later the BF.2b. He and his observers accounted for twenty-four enemy aircraft. However, on 2 December he was shot down by Walter von Bülow, leader of *Jasta 36* and, although his observer on this occasion survived as a prisoner, Harry Luchford MC and Bar did not.

Lt Walter von Bülow-Bothkamp had been with a Saxon hussar regiment, known as the 'Death's Head (*Totenkopf*) Hussars' in 1915. Once with the Aviation Service, he flew with two two-seater units, one operating in Palestine. By the time he joined *Jasta 18* in France he had four victories to his name. In May 1917 he took command of *Jasta 36* and rapidly brought his score to twenty-eight on 2 December, bringing down Harry Luchford of 20 Squadron on that day, and he had received the *Pour le Mérite*. Given command of *Jasta Boelcke* on 13 December, he had not added to his score before falling in combat on 6 January 1918, his Albatros D.V actually falling inside Allied lines.

Bülow was shot down and credited to two British air fighters, W. M. Fry MC, flying a Spad with 23 Squadron, and F. G Quigley MC in a Camel of 70 Squadron. The image is of Willie Fry standing in front of his Spad. He had started his war in the infantry but, being under age, still 17, was sent home. Transferring to the RFC he became a pilot and flew with 12 and 11 Squadrons. One flight of the latter became 60 Squadron in 1917, flying Nieuport Scouts and that summer he scored five victories before moving to 23 Squadron, bringing his score to ten. With the award of the MC he returned to England but managed to persuade his superiors to allow him back to active duty, being sent to 87 Squadron, which was preparing for France in 1918. Before it did so, Fry was posted to 79 Squadron, and with this unit he shot down a Fokker Triplane on 11 May, his final victory. He remained in the RAF reaching the rank of wing commander before retiring but he served again in the Second World War. Willie died in 1992.

Francis Quigley came from Toronto and started the war as an engineer. Once he became a pilot he joined 70 Squadron and soon rose to be one of its stars, claiming nine victories by the end of 1917; the share of the von Bülow shoot-down on 6 January 1918 was his eleventh. In the early months of 1918 he really got into his stride, and by March his score was thirty-three. He already had the MC and Bar, and added the DSO, but received an ankle wound on 27 March and returned to England and then went back to Canada as an instructor. Returning to England that September, he was struck down by the influenza pandemic aboard ship and, two days after arriving at Liverpool, died; he was twenty-four.

Captain F. G. Quigley MC seated in a captured Pfalz D.III Scout. The Pfalz came to the front in late 1917 and supplemented gaps in several *Jastas*. The D.III and the improved D.IIIa remained in action during the early summer of 1918, by which time the Fokker D.VII fighters were equipping most German units.

Ernst Hess had learned to fly pre-war and once the war really started he was flying Fokkers on both the British and French fronts, at one stage with Boelcke and Immelmann in *FA62*. After a period as an instructor he was posted to *Jasta 28w*, where he brought his score to fourteen by September, and was given command of *Jasta 19*. With a score of seventeen, he was shot down by *Adjutant* de Kergolay of French *Escadrille N94* on 23 December. It was the Frenchman's first victory.

Max Müller started his service life as a driver and also as a chauffeur for the Bavarian war minister. Every time he opened the door to him, Müller would request a transfer to aviation. By late 1913 he got his wish and his Bavarian Pilot's Badge in April 1914. Soon after war began he broke both legs in a crash, but upon recovery went back to his two-seater unit, running up a total of 160 missions by May 1916. With several awards, it was not difficult to transfer to fighters and he joined *Jasta 2*, under Boelcke. By the end of 1916 he had achieved five victories and in 1917 went to *Jasta 28w*. By the autumn his score had reached twenty-nine. He returned to his former unit to help Erwin Böhme improve a particularly lean period for the *Jasta* but when von Bülow, who had taken over the *Jasta* after Böhme's death, was lost Müller took command. Before adding to his score of thirty-six he was shot down and killed attacking an RE.8 two-seater on 9 January 1918. With his Albatros on fire he jumped rather than burn. He had received the Blue Max and the Bavarian Knight's Cross of the Military Max-Joseph Order, making him Ritter von Müller.

Albatros D.V Scouts of *Jasta 23b* on Faureiul airfield in March 1918. The white painted sign in the foreground reads: 'All horses and wheel traffic strictly prohibited'.

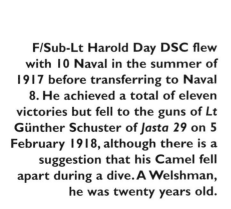

This picture is of Otto Kissenberth who saw combat in 1916 and 1917, commanding *Jasta 23b* for most of this period. However, having brought his score to twenty on 16 May 1918, whilst flying a cross-marked captured Sopwith Camel, he was seriously injured flying the British machine on 29 May. He is seen here in front of the Camel. Bavarian-born Kissenberth was, nevertheless, awarded the Blue Max whilst in hospital in July 1918. Surviving the war, he died in a mountaineering fall on 2 August 1919.

F/Sub-Lt Harold Day DSC flew with 10 Naval in the summer of 1917 before transferring to Naval 8. He achieved a total of eleven victories but fell to the guns of *Lt* Günther Schuster of *Jasta 29* on 5 February 1918, although there is a suggestion that his Camel fell apart during a dive. A Welshman, he was twenty years old.

F/Cdr Guy Price came from Dublin and following a period with 13 Naval Squadron moved to Naval 8. In December 1917 he claimed five victories, two shared with Harry Day, and in 1918 brought his score to twelve. The Camel squadrons were increasingly flying ground-attack sorties and on one such operation on 18 February he was caught by Theodore Rumpel of *Jasta 23b* and killed. He had received the DSC and Bar.

Coming from a small town near Hamburg, Theodore Rumpel had begun his war with a *Jäger* regiment on the Eastern Front, being commissioned in May 1916. In August he applied for pilot training and began war flying on two-seaters. With a transfer to fighters, he went to *Jasta 16b*, then transferred to *Jasta 23b*. Guy Price was his fifth victory, but he was badly wounded in an air battle on 24 March. He became an instructor and in the Second World War was commander of Dulag Luft transit camp, through which the majority of Allied airmen prisoners passed. Note the wooden ladder for ease of climbing into the Albatros cockpit.

Hans Klein, on the right, in conversation with Manfred von Richthofen. Stettin-born, Bethge was with the infantry before moving to aviation. He first saw fighter action with *Kek* Vaux in summer 1916 and the following year was posted to *Jasta 4*. With this unit he brought his score to twenty-two by 30 November, and received the Blue Max. A senior member of *JGI* he was wounded in action on 19 February 1918, in a fight with Camels, losing a thumb. He remained with *JGI* until the war's end as a ground officer. In the Second World War he served with the *Luftwaffe* but was killed in 1944.

Hauptmann Rudolf Berthold, a northern Bavarian, had been with an infantry regiment from 1910 but then decided to join the air service, which he did in 1913. Becoming an observer he flew two-seaters until he applied for pilot training. He became one of the early Fokker pilots, flying with *Kek* Vaux but, after scoring five victories, he was injured in a crash in April 1916. It was the first of many wounds and injuries he would receive in the war. However, these setbacks rarely kept him away from battle. When *Jasta 4* was formed from his old *Kek* he joined it, and in October was given command of *Jasta 16b*. With a score of twelve he was shot down on 23 May 1917 and in the crash received a fractured skull, broken pelvis, thigh and nose. Back in the fight by August he commanded *Jasta 18* and by the end of the year had a score of twenty-eight victories, and the *Pour le Mérite*. In October he was wounded again, a bullet smashing his right upper arm. In March 1918 Berthold was given command of *JGII*, a position he held until wounded once more on 10 August. His victories numbered forty-four. In 1919 he joined the *Freikorps* during the post-war revolution in Germany but was killed by rioters on 15 March 1920. This picture was taken while he was an observer, shown by the observer flying badge just above his belt. The Iron Cross 1st and 2nd Class are shown.

Oberleutnant Hans-Joachim Buddecke was another pre-war soldier, having served from 1910 to 1912 before working for his uncle in the USA, where, buying his own aeroplane, he taught himself to fly. Once the war began and he was back in Germany, he started flying two-seaters in France, but in 1916 he was serving in Turkey on fighters. He had considerable success and by the end of 1916 had ten combat victories. After a brief spell back in France he returned to the Middle East. Returning to France once more, he was with *Jasta 18* but was shot down while saving his leader, Rudolf Berthold, in a fight on 10 March. He fell to the guns of 3 Naval Squadron. He had received the Blue Max for his prowess in the Middle East, rather than an individual score of victories.

Australian Captain G. F. Hughes was a successful BF.2b pilot in early 1918, winning the MC and gaining, with his observers, eleven victories. On 13 March, he, with Captain H. Claye in the back cockpit, downed Lothar von Richthofen, who was badly injured in the resultant crash and out of action for some months. The victory was shared with Camel pilot A. H. Orlebar of 73 Squadron.

The Sopwith Dolphin began to appear on the Western Front in early 1918 as the
French Spads were withdrawn from RFC service. It had an in-line engine rather than
the usual rotary engines of Sopwith machines. It also had a back-stagger top wing
arrangement with an open space where normally a centre section would have been.
As this picture shows, early versions carried two Vickers guns firing through the
propeller and two upward-pointing Lewis guns. The Dolphin equipped four front-line
squadrons in 1918. A good all-round fighting machine, it was especially useful engaging
high-flying German reconnaissance machines.

There were a good many NCO pilots on active duty in the First World War. This picture is of Sgt E. J. Elton DCM MM who, along with his gunners, claimed sixteen victories in just over a month during February and March 1918, on BF.2bs of 22 Squadron. Earlier in the war, as a mechanic in 6 Squadron, he had helped Lanoe Hawker design the gun mounting on a Bristol Scout. His prowess was also recognised by the Italian Government, who awarded him their *Bronze Medal (Medaglio di Bronzo al Valore Militaire)*.

This is F/Sgt E. J. Elton in his BF.2b. While his gunner had twin Lewis guns to help defend the aircraft, Elton mounted another Lewis gun on the top wing, in addition to his Vickers gun. The mounting shows the top gun could be fixed to fire forward over the propeller, but could also be pulled down to fire upwards. Ordinarily, the observer needed to be rather strong to swing and fire twin Lewis guns and many observers were more than content to use just one.

Augustus Henry Orlebar scored seven victories in the First World War but with three different squadrons and aircraft. He fought in France and Gallipoli with the Army before being wounded by a Turkish sniper. Back in England he became a pilot and, going to 19 Squadron, was credited with two victories flying Spads. Moving to Camels with 73 Squadron, he shot down four more while, late in 1918, he flew Snipes with 43 Squadron with whom he downed victory number eight. Remaining in the RAF he was part of Britain's Schneider Trophy team between 1929 and 1931, and in the Second World War commanded RAF Northolt fighter base. He died in 1943 from bone cancer of the jaw.

Adolf von Tutschek flew this distinctive Fokker Dr.I leading *JGII* in early 1918 with normal drab-green colouring with a black tail and rudder. He was shot down in this aircraft on 15 March 1918 and, although he appeared to have force-landed safely, was found dead next to his machine as ground troops reached him.

Tutschek sitting on the cockpit edge of his penultimate victory, number twenty-six, on 5 March 1918. SE.5A (C1057) from 24 Squadron, its pilot was captured. Tutschek is demonstrating how the wing Lewis gun could be pulled towards the pilot, both for upward firing, and for changing an ammunition drum. The drum here is not in place, and note the different design of the Vickers' gun-sight.

It was H. B. Redler of 24 Squadron whose fire caught von Tutschek on 15 March. Although the German ace appeared to be unharmed, except for what appeared to be a graze from a bullet, he had died at the scene of his forced landing. This picture shows Harold Redler seated in a Nieuport Scout of 40 Squadron in 1917, the unit in which he served alongside Edward Mannock. He claimed three victories with 40, and a further six with 24. Sadly, after leaving 24 Squadron, he was killed in a flying accident at Turnberry in a DH.9, on 21 June 1918. Note the flight leader's pennant attached to the wing struts.

Hans Bethge achieved twenty victories with *Jasta 1* and *Jasta 30* between August 1916 and March 1918. He too had been nominated for the Blue Max but his death on 17 March during an attack on a British two-seater meant it did not proceed. He was flying a Pfalz D.III on this day. His body was taken home to Berlin for burial. He was 27 years old and had flown with von Richthofen in *BAO* in 1916.

Captain St C. C. Tayler MC scored four victories with a DH.5 of 32 Squadron in 1917 and, in early 1918, commanded a flight of Camels within 80 Squadron. In March that year he brought his overall score to ten but was shot down and killed in a fight with *Jasta 24* on the 17th. He was claimed by Heinrich Kroll. Although born in Winchester, he had spent much of his early life in Natal, South Africa.

Heinrich Claudius Kroll's early war service was with the infantry, where he was commissioned and decorated before moving to the Air Service. On the French front he flew Rumpler two-seaters before moving to fighters. His first fighting unit was *Jasta 9*, and his fifth victory was over the French ace René Dorme on 1 May 1917 – his own first kill. Later that year he moved to command *Jasta 24* although, before he achieved anything, he was shot down in flames by Clive Warman, an American with the RFC. Fortunately he survived the experience and continued to lead his *Jasta*, won the *Pour le Mérite* and achieved a total of thirty-three victories by August 1918. A bad wound on the 14th ended his combat career.

Clive Warman, from Norfolk, Virginia, transferred to the RFC from the Canadian infantry and, once a pilot, began flying Spads with 23 Squadron. In a little over two months in 1917 he claimed twelve victories, winning both the MC and DSO before suffering a wound that put him out of action. Surviving the war he was killed in a flying accident while serving with No. 1 Squadron, Canadian Air Force, over north London, in an Avro, on 12 June 1919.

The former British airfield at Léchelle in April 1918. It had been over-run by the German advance which began in March and was now the home of *JGI*, its Triplanes clearly in view in front of RFC Bessonneau hangars. Note the airman viewing activity over the lines with his long-range binoculars. The Triplanes have the new Latin crosses on them, the *pattée* crosses having been phased out.

Younger brother of James McCudden, John Anthony 'Jack' McCudden flew SE.5s with 84 Squadron. He achieved eight victories and received the MC in 1918, although his first two victories were gained flying DH.4 bombers with 25 Squadron in the autumn of 1917. He was shot down and killed by *Lt* Hans Wolff of *Jasta 11* on 18 March and buried at St Souplet the next day. He was 20 years old.

Rudolf 'Rudi' Windisch, seated in his Fokker D.VII with its distinctive stag motif. A former infantryman, he had been with Boelcke in 1916 but in 1917 began to fly with *Jasta 32b*, were he scored five victories. In early 1918 he was commanding *Jasta 66* on the French front, bringing his overall score to twenty-two by 27 May, but was then brought down behind the French lines. It was thought he had been captured, and so his nomination for the *Pour le Mérite* progressed and was awarded on 6 June. However, he had not survived, the circumstances not having been confirmed, other than it was suggested he was shot trying to escape. Note the unusual telescopic gun-sight and the face-rest.

Losing a limb did not prohibit a man serving in the air services in the First World War and Sydney Carlin is a case in point. A Yorkshireman from Hull, he had won the DCM with the Royal Engineers in 1915 and was commissioned. The following year he was wounded and lost a leg, but received the Military Cross. Joining the RFC, where he was known as 'Timbertoes', he found himself with 74 Squadron in May 1918 and before he was brought down and captured on 21 September had shot down five German aircraft and five balloons, to receive the DFC. In the Second World War he flew as an air gunner before being killed during an air raid on his aerodrome in 1941.

Major K. L. 'Grid' Caldwell MC DFC, from New Zealand, flew with 60 Squadron in 1917 before commanding 74 Squadron in 1918. On one occasion during a patrol he and Sydney Carlin collided in mid-air and were lucky to survive. Keith Caldwell had achieved nine victories with 60, adding a further sixteen with 74. He later became an air commodore in the RNZAF and in 1945 was AOC, RNZAF HQ in London, for which he was made CBE. He died in 1980.

Chapter 5
1918

In many ways 1917 had been the defining period of development in air fighting and the fighting pilots, especially the aces, had become established. It could be said that 1918 was just more of the same, although naturally there are several aspects to be considered.

The first was the massive German attack which began on 21 March, known as Operation MICHAEL. With the ending of the war in Russia, Germany suddenly had a vast increase in troops and this, coupled with the knowledge that with America now in the war, and knowing that the Allies would also have an increase in manpower, prompted them to attack in force. It began from just north of Arras down to the south of Noyon. The Germans re-launched their offensive several times over, under different codenames such as GEORGE, GEORGETTE. BLÜCHER, GNEISENAU, and HAGEN, but were fought to a standstill, even though the original attack had gained a considerable surprise advantage. The fact that a large number of German troops stopped to loot alcohol stores to the point that they could hardly stand, let alone advance farther, is only part of the story. Like so many offensives in the First World War, while the idea was always to push the enemy back, it rarely happened and when it did, as in March 1918, there was insufficient back-up to consolidate gains made. Another German push on the Armentières front was also an initial success in April, while the French were forced back towards the end of May. The Germans being unable to keep up the pressure, the British and French gradually recaptured lost territory, and from then on, starting with a major offensive, led by the BEF, finally brought about Germany's surrender. That offensive began with the Battle of Amiens on 8 August and is known as the 'Hundred Days' although it was really ninety-six days.

It was during this March period that the British fighter squadrons harried more and more German troops and transport on the ground. All fighter units were encouraged in this regard but especially the Sopwith Camel units, that also carried four 20lb Cooper bombs. RFC two-seater ground attack squadrons were flying support missions, especially against trench systems, gun emplacements and strongpoints.

Another event at this time was the amalgamation of the RNAS and RFC into the Royal Air Force on 1 April 1918. This changed little of note in France and the war went on.

American troops had already started to arrive in France, along with the USAS – United States Air Service – and were attached to the French. However, they had no aircraft and had to rely on what the French gave them. Their first fighter squadrons were equipped with the Nieuport 28, a machine the French, strangely, did not use themselves. The first two units were the 94th and 95th Pursuit Squadrons. Also somewhat different was the armament layout, two Vickers guns offset on the left-hand side on top of the forward fuselage.

On 14 April Lieutenants Doug Campbell and Alan Winslow of the 94th shot down two German fighters to open the American account. Douglas Campbell would go on to claim six German aircraft before being wounded on 5 June. The *Escadrille Lafayette* had been incorporated into the USAS to become the 103rd Aero Squadron. Raoul Lufbery, promoted to major, joined the 94th Aero and claimed a victory on 12 April, which might have proved the Americans' first, but it went unconfirmed. Another was similarly unconfirmed on 27 April. Then, on 18 May, while attacking a German two-seater, Lufbery's Nieuport was set on fire and he took the quickest way out by jumping. He had not increased his score of sixteen achieved with the *Lafayette*.

The pilot who was to become the American top ace, Edward Rickenbacker, achieved his first victory flying with the 94th on 29 April. He would go on to claim twenty-six victories by the end of October.

There were some American pilots serving with the RAF, men who had come to England prior to the USAS, and had trained in England, and a fighter squadron was formed within the ranks of the RAF – the 148th Aero. Several others had been distributed among various RAF squadrons, prior to a number of them transferring to American squadrons. Among them was Elliot White Springs, whose post-war books on flying made his name. Lawrence Callahan started out with 85 Squadron, along with Springs, and both moved to the 148th Aero. Springs gained sixteen victories, Callahan five. Field Kindley shot down his first German with 65 Squadron RAF, adding eleven more with the 148th. George Vaughn Jr claimed seven victories with 84 Squadron, flying SE.5s, then a further six flying Camels with the US 17th Aero.

Several aces remained with RAF squadrons. Wilfred Beaver flew BF.2b machines with 20 Squadron and, between November 1917 and June 1918, achieved nineteen victories. Fred 'Razors' Gillet flew Sopwith Dolphins with 79 Squadron, claiming twenty victories. The Iaccaci brothers, August and Paul, both with 20 Squadron, were each credited with seventeen kills. Howard Kullberg gained nineteen victories with No. 1 Squadron, on SE.5s, Bill Lambert eighteen victories with 24 Squadron and Oren Rose, 92 Squadron, sixteen victories.

Many volunteers who flew with the French, generally via the *Lafayette* Flying Corps (it was called a Corps because there were too many volunteers for a single squadron), remained with them. Among the more successful were Frank Baylies, twelve victories, with the Storks, Tom Cassady, five and three probables with *Spa163*, then a further four with the US 28th Aero. Another who scored with the Storks was Edwin Parsons, who had eight victories with *N124* and *Spa3*. Then there was David Putnam who had a fascinating career from early 1918. Flying with *MS156* he scored four victories but with nine probables. Moving to *Spa38* he shot down five more plus seven probables. Finally, transferring to the USAS, he gained four and one probable with the 139th Aero before falling in combat on 12 September, shot down by Georg von Hantelmann of *Jasta 15*.

Two outstanding Belgian pilots were Willy Coppens and Andre Demeulemeester. Both had begun scoring in 1917 but Coppens became something of a phenomenon. As already mentioned, balloons were very dangerous targets and most top aces left them well alone. Coppens, on the other hand, couldn't keep away. By March 1918 he had achieved four probable victories over aeroplanes, then a fighter on 25 April. By the time he was seriously wounded attacking a balloon on 14 October his score of victories totalled thirty-seven, but thirty-five were balloons! It cost him his left leg, but he was made a baron by a grateful country.

Demeulemeester scored a total of just eleven victories, with just one, his final kill, being a balloon on 5 October 1918. However, he had claimed sixteen more that were only credited as probables. Both pilots flew Hanriot HD.1 machines, a French machine rejected by the French, but also used by the Italians.

The top three French aces with high scores against balloons were: Léon Bourjade with twenty-seven, Michel Coiffard with twenty-four and Maurice Boyau with twenty-one. Bourjade flew with *Spa152* and ended the war with twenty-eight victories, all but one being balloons. He later became a missionary but died in 1924. Coiffard scored thirty-four kills in all, so ten were aeroplanes, all with *Spa124*. He died of injuries received in combat on 28 October. Boyau's final score was thirty-five, all while flying with *Spa77*, but he was killed in action on 16 September, claimed by Georg von Hantelmann, who, as mentioned above, shot down David Putnam.

The two top German aces against balloons were Friedrich Ritter von Röth and Heinrich Gontermann, with twenty and eighteen respectively. 'Fritz' Röth achieved twenty-eight victories and the *Pour le Mérite* and, of his balloon kills, he claimed four on 1 April 1918 and five on 29 May, both times in one sortie. Even when he began his first three balloons on 25 January were all flamed in eight minutes. Shattered by Germany's defeat he shot himself on New Year's Day 1919. Gontermann was long dead by this time, having been killed in a Fokker Dr.I crash on 30 October 1917; his score was thirty-nine victories, including eighteen balloons.

Anthony Beauchamp Proctor, a South African, flew with 84 Squadron in 1918 and achieved fifty-four victories. He, too, got the balloon-bug for among his score were sixteen balloons, although his first, on 1 June, was his twenty-second claim. Awarded the VC, DSO, and DFC he was killed in a flying accident on 21 June 1921. Before leaving the matter of balloons the name of Frank Luke Jr must be recorded.

Frank Luke, from Phoenix, Arizona, had joined the US 27th Aero in July 1918, in fact on the same day Edward Mannock was killed (see below). At first he laboured under something of a cloud because his first claim seemed suspect to his superiors. Luke was somewhat of a loner and this made him even more rebellious, but he soon began to record confirmed victories, mostly over balloons. On 12 September he flamed his first and nine more followed by the 18th, plus two Fokker biplanes and a two-seater. By the 29th he had shot down four aircraft and fourteen balloons, which, together with his heroic last stand, produced a posthumous Medal of Honor. However, on that fateful 29th, after flaming three balloons, he was brought down by ground fire. Although he survived a crash landing, and had been wounded, he did not give up and began firing at approaching German soldiers with his sidearm, but their return fire ended the 21 year old's life.

* *

The year 1918 saw some of the greatest aces fall, but not always in air combat. Perhaps the best known occurred on 21 April, Baron Manfred von Richthofen being brought down by ground fire and killed. He had eighty victories, the highest score in any of the belligerent nations.

Although the vast majority of airmen shot down were new to the battle front, experience gained over a long period held no guarantee of a long life. On 1 June the veteran Reggie Dallas, now commanding No. 40 Squadron, was killed. From time to time, squadron commanders were refused permission to cross the front lines, although many of the more aggressive ones did. However, on this day, Dallas was flying just inside Allied territory but was surprised by three Fokker Triplanes of *Jasta 14*. Johann Werner, its CO, managed to surprise the Australian in his SE.5 and he crashed to his death. A similar fate befell another former RNAS pilot, Charles Booker, on 13 August. Commanding 201 Squadron, he had just shot down his twenty-ninth German aeroplane but saw one of his pilots in trouble with some Fokker D.VIIs. He immediately went to his aid. In doing so he was killed by Ulrich Neckel of *Jasta 19*, his twenty-second victory.

On 9 July the great James McCudden was killed in a flying accident on his way to take command of 60 Squadron. That month also saw the demise of Edward Mannock DSO MC on 26 July. He and one of his men had just brought down a German two-seater and Mannock, CO of 85 Squadron, knew that standing orders mentioned that a pilot returning from a patrol with ammunition remaining should fire into Pacault Wood, just north of la Bassée canal. Having seen his final victim go down Mannock, already fairly low, fired into the wood, which was known to be full of German soldiers. However, ground fire hit the SE.5 which crashed on fire, and Mannock, victor of some sixty combats, perished. George McElroy, flying with 24 Squadron, was killed in similar circumstances five days later. His final victory was not confirmed, except that the Germans, in dropping a note about his death, said McElroy had just brought down a German two-seater, which would have been his forty-seventh kill. McElroy was 25 years old, Mannock 31. Both are buried in

Laventie cemetery, although Mannock's headstone does not bear his name, just 'A British Airman of the Great War'. They were friends in war and remain so in death.

* *

By this time, the main German fighter on the Western Front was the Fokker D.VII biplane, a machine that would have become even more feared than it was if the cream of the German fighter force had not already fallen or been moved away from the front. The Fokker Triplane had all but disappeared, although a few still existed on some *Jastas*, along with Albatros and Pfalz Scouts. Among the pilots still insisting on flying the Triplane was Josef Jacobs of *Jasta 7*.

From slow beginnings in 1916 on two-seaters and then Fokker Eindeckers, he began to blossom with *Jasta 22* in 1917 and by the end of that year had twelve victories. Given command of *Jasta 7*, Jacobs flew a black Triplane and, although his unit equipped with biplanes, Jacobs much preferred his Triplane; in fact he had two personal machines. He also flew other *staffel* machines but preferred to use the Triplane when operating at lower altitudes where it generally out-performed RAF aircraft; his overall score of forty-eight included some thirty whilst in a Triplane. This was many more than any other Triplane pilot. Richthofen, for example, while his name is synonymous with the Triplane, only achieved nineteen kills in it. With other *Jasta* aircraft now all using in-line Mercedes engines, Jacobs needed to locate replacement rotary engines, and front-line troops were asked to report any British rotary-engined machines down inside German lines, where engines could be salvaged.

* *

For the remainder of the war, as the early German offensive advances were gradually rolled back, it became a relentless retreat for the Germans from 8 August. While the *Jasta* pilots were still a force to contend with, the RAF, French Air Force and the USAS were overwhelming opponents. Their bombing machines constantly attacked German rear areas, supply dumps and transport; artillery observation was now down to a fine art by both aircraft and balloon observers; and fighters dominated above and beyond the trenches, engaging anything that the Germans put up against them.

One surprise for the Allied airmen, but especially for the fighter pilots, was the introduction of BMW engines for the Fokker D.VIIs. Until the summer of 1918 the D.VII had a Mercedes engine, but the BMW gave the machine much more power, but looked no different – until a combat began. However, the Allied pilots were quick to adapt.

Ever so gradually the Allied armies advanced: 8 August became known as the Black Day for the German army and, as much as anything, it was continual harassment from the air that really began to demoralise the men on the ground. It was combined arms action, in which the British excelled above all others and included tanks, highly-mobile artillery, infantry in APCs – the first ever; and air re-supply, 1st Royal Irish Fusiliers being the first troops ever re-supplied by air while in action. All this combined with aerial reconnaissance and improved artillery observation with more reliable radios allowing better communication between air and ground; aircraft co-operated with ground troops by bombing and strafing.

Just one more fighter arrived in France, the Sopwith Snipe, but it arrived too late in the war to equip more than a couple of squadrons, namely, Nos 43 and 201, that swopped them for their Camels.

American troops also advanced along with the French at St Mihel and the Meuse-Argonne in September while, in the north, Belgium began to be liberated. Seeing the end, the German Kaiser fled to Holland on 10 November, Armistice terms were signed and the guns fell silent at 11.00am on the 11th.

Three stalwarts of the 94th Aero Squadron, United States Air Service, in front of a Nieuport 28. Eddie Rickenbacker is on the left and would become the top American ace. Doug Campbell is in the centre, who scored one of the unit's first two victories, and Ken Marr, who had flown with the French and later became the CO of the 94th, is on the right.

Elliott White Springs served with the RAF initially, flying with 85 Squadron on SE.5s. Later he moved to the Camel-equipped 148th Aero, ending the war with sixteen combat victories and the DSC. He died in 1959.

George Vaughn flew SE.5s with the RAF's 84 Squadron, gaining seven victories, before moving to the 17th Aero. On 14 October 1918 he scored his thirteenth victory and had been awarded both the British DFC and the American DSC. He remained with aviation circles post-war and in later life was an active member of the American Fighter Aces Association until his death in 1989.

Field Kindley was another American to fly with the RAF, in Camels of 65 Squadron, then with the American 148th Aero. In total, he had twelve victories and the DSC and Oak Leaf. In February 1920 he took command of the US 94th Aero in Texas but was killed in a flying accident on 1 February.

An American who remained with the RAF in 1918 was F. W. Gillet, who was known as 'Razors'. He flew Sopwith Dolphins with 79 Squadron and achieved twenty victories by the Armistice, and been awarded the DFC and Bar, plus the Belgian *Croix de Guerre*. Fred Gillet died in 1969.

The two Iaccaci brothers were unique in that they both flew **Bristol Fighters** with the **RAF**, both scored seventeen victories, both received the **DFC**, and both survived. This portrait is Paul, born in 1890 and died in 1965.

August Iaccaci was born in 1893 and died in 1980. He had just been posted to another BF.2b Squadron as a flight commander but a slight eye wound ended his war flying.

Howard Kullberg flew SE.5s with the RAF's No. I Squadron in 1918, and was credited with nineteen victories and won the DFC, before being wounded in September. Post-war he became involved in civil flying but was killed in a flying accident on 5 August 1924 while instructing a student pilot.

William C. Lambert had his first experience of flight in 1910, aged 17, on a joy-ride at the 4th of July celebrations in his native Ohio. He joined the RFC in Canada in 1915 and, following training, was posted to 24 Squadron in France to fly SE.5s. He gained eighteen victories and the DFC before fatigue overtook him. His score is sometimes quoted as high as twenty-two. He died in March 1982.

Does it say anything about the USAS that so many trained flyers preferred to remain with either the RAF or French Air Force rather than transferring? Another to remain *in situ* was Oren J. Rose. Flying SE.5s with 92 Squadron in 1918 he gained sixteen victories in the last six months of the war, and received both the DFC and Bar. Post-war he served with the RAF in Russia, and in the Second World War again served, this time in the USAAF. He died in June 1971.

American Frank Baylies sailed to France in 1916 to work with the US Ambulance Service, seeing active duty at Verdun and the Argonne before moving to Serbia, where he won the *Croix de Guerre*. Being taken for a flight in May 1917 convinced him to learn to fly, which eventually led him to *Spa3* of the *Storks Group* later that year. In the first five months of 1918 he downed twelve German aircraft before being killed in combat with *Jasta 19* on 17 June. He received the *Médaille Militaire* but had refused a captaincy with the USAS to remain with the French.

Tom Cassady also served with the Ambulance Service before learning to fly, then flew with *Spa157* in late 1917. Transferring to the USAS he was assigned to the French *Spa163* and achieved five victories and three probables before moving to the 28th Aero, bringing his score to nine. He received the American DSC and Oak Leaf to add to his French *Legion d'Honneur* and *Croix de Guerre* with three *Palmes* and one *Étoile*. In the Second World War he worked with the French Resistance and the OSS. He also helped with the planning of the landings in southern France and, following the liberation of Paris, was put in charge of all intelligence personnel. He died in July 1972.

David Putnam was an American who had a varied flying career with the French in 1918, with *MS156* and *Spa38*. Before his transfer to the US 139th Aero he had accounted for eight aircraft and a balloon and been awarded the *Médaille Militaire* and *Croix de Guerre*. With the USAS he added four more victories to bring his score to thirteen but had also been credited with at least seventeen probables. He died in combat with *Jasta 15* on 12 September, claimed by Georg von Hantelmann. At the war's end the French bestowed upon him the *Legion d'Honneur*, and in 1919 his own country awarded him a posthumous DSC.

Georg von Hantelmann was one of the youngest German aces, with twenty-five victories by the war's end, flying with *Jasta 15*. On 12 September he downed David Putnam of the 139th Aero. Although recommended for the *Blue Max*, it had not been approved by the Armistice. Surviving the war, he was murdered by Polish poachers on the family estate in East Prussia in September 1924. This picture shows him in front of his Fokker D.VII with a laurel wreath on its front and the number 20, denoting his twentieth victory, which he achieved on 9 October 1918.

Willy Coppens, the Belgian ace, in front of a Hanriot HD.1 with its *9me Escadrille* marking of a thistle. Coppens was credited with thirty-seven combat victories, thirty-five of them being kite balloons. Badly wounded on 14 October 1918, he lost his left leg, but he was made a baron after the war, remaining in service until 1940, mainly as an air attaché. In the Second World War he was living in Switzerland but was active in resistance work. He died in 1986.

P5/16   Andre Demeulemeester, left, and Georges Kervyn de Lettenhove in front of their Nieuport 23 Scouts. Andre claimed eleven victories, with sixteen more unconfirmed, and survived the war. Georges was officially credited with four victories and had another nine unconfirmed. Both flew with *Ime* and *9me Escadrilles*. They died in 1973 and 1979 respectively. The Nieuport on the right is the one used by Georges, with the name 'Vampire' on the fuselage, in red, edged blue. Andre's in the foreground had yellow top decking and a yellow square on the fuselage on which was painted a red outline figure.

Top French destroyer of balloons was Léon Bourjade who flew with *Spa152*. A former artilleryman, he moved to aviation in 1917 and flamed his first gas-bag on 27 May 1918. His final victory – his twenty-eighth – came on 29 October, all but one being balloons. After the war he became a missionary but died in October 1924 in British New Guinea, having been ordained as a priest. It is believed he died of leprosy.

Michel Coiffard achieved thirty-four victories with *Spa154* in 1918, twenty-four being balloons. Wounded on 28 October, he succumbed to his injuries the next day. He received the *Legion d'Honneur, Médaille Militaire* and *Croix de Guerre* to which was added the British Military Cross. Before becoming a pilot, he had been with the French artillery, being wounded on no less than six occasions between 1914 and 1916.

Another French balloon-buster was Maurice Bouau, flying with *Spa77*. His final score was thirty-five, of which twenty-one were balloons. He was shot down and killed by *Jasta 15*'s Georg von Hantelmann on 6 September 1918.

Karl Schlegal, a Saxon, flew with *Jasta 45* in 1918, achieving twenty-two victories, fourteen of which were balloons. He had been in line for the Blue Max but his death in combat on 27 October ended the process. He had shot down a balloon and an aircraft on this day but these were not made official due to his loss. He was shot down by Pierre Marionovitch of *Spa94*.

Among the British balloon aces was Henry Woollett of 43 Squadron. His first balloon kill was his fourteenth, but by the war's end he had scored thirty-five victories, eleven of them balloons. By August 1918 he had received the DSO and Bar, MC and Bar, and the French awarded him their *Legion d'Honneur* and *Croix de Guerre* after hostilities. He remained in the RAF post-war and died in October 1969.

A line-up of 43 Squadron's Camels, with Woollett's D6402 in the foreground, in which he scored twenty-three of his victories. Note the unusual red, white and blue horizontal lines on the tail fin, his flight commander marking. The individual letter 'S' is marked on the top fuselage decking. On 12 April, in this machine, he claimed a total of six German aircraft shot down.

Sous-lieutenant Pierre Marionovitch of *Spa94* was the son of a Serbian diplomat working in Paris, while his mother was Polish. Living in France he joined the flying service in 1916 and was sent to *N48* but then became ill. Once recovered, he was posted to *N94* and by the end of 1917 had three victories. By the Armistice his score had reached twenty-one, plus three probables. One of the youngest aces, at 19½, he received the *Legion d'Honneur, Medaille Militaire and Croix de Guerre with* fourteen *Palmes.* Note the badge above his *Medaille Militaire,* a running skeleton carrying a scythe, the insignia of *N94.* Marionovitch was killed in a flying accident at Brussels, Evere, airfield on 2 September 1919. He is buried in the Père Lachaise Cemetery in Paris, next to the grave of Oscar Wilde. Two of his paternal uncles were in the Russian artillery.

The grave of Pierre Marionovitch, Paris.

Gustav Fraedrich of *Jasta 72* being helped into his parachute harness in July 1918. Only German airmen were issued parachutes during 1918; although not obligatory, a number of them were used and saved the wearer's life. Fraedrich achieved five victories with *Jasta 72* in 1918, to add to a single victory scored whilst serving with *FA30* in 1917.

Friedrich 'Fritz' Röth of *Jasta 23* and *16b*
was another balloon ace, with twenty of
twenty-eight kills being gas-bags. Wound
in the artillery in 1915 he moved to
aviation and was badly injured in a flying
accident but upon recovery he eventual
found himself with *Jasta 23b* after a peri
on two-seaters. He claimed ten victorie:
but one balloons, four in one day – 1 Ap
the day the RAF was born. Given comm
of *Jasta 16b*, he opened his account on 2
May with five balloons in one sortie. He
received the *Pour le Mérite* and his final
victory came on 14 October but he was
wounded in the foot on this date. Shatte
by Germany losing the war, Röthe
committed suicide on New Year's Eve. H
body, with a gunshot wound to the temp
was found on the railway line between E
and Nüremberg. The picture shows Rötl
the right, with Eduard von Schleich, lead
of *Jagdgruppe 8,* and victor of thirty-five
combats.

The mercurial Frank Luke Jr of the US 27th Aero who claimed eighteen victories in
September 1918, fourteen of which were balloons. Despite being in combat for so short a
time, his achievements produced the DSC and Oak Leaf Cluster, and a posthumous Medal of
Honor. Killed in action on 29 September, he was 21 years of age.

George McElroy was badly gassed in 1915 while serving with the Royal Irish Regiment and sent on garrison duty. Wanting to return to active duty he joined the RFC and flew SE.5s with 40 Squadron at the end of 1917. Throughout the spring and early summer of 1918 he amassed an astonishing forty-six victories and received the MC and two Bars, then the DFC and Bar. On 31 July he failed to return, his squadron later learning that he had shot down a two-seater over the front but had fallen to ground fire and been killed.

Ernst Udet, second highest scoring German pilot of the First World War. His tally by September 1918 was sixty-two before being wounded on the 26th. He too received the *Pour le Mérite*. Post-war he became famous as a stunt flyer, also flying in American movies. In the Second World War he served in the *Luftwaffe* but, being unable to cope with political infighting, committed suicide in November 1941.

Three German aces from two different services. On the left is Josef Jacobs, forty-eight victories between 1916 and 1918, many flying the Fokker Triplane long after it had ceased to be a major front-line fighter. His two companions were both *Marine* fighter pilots, Gottard Sachsenberg who ended the war with thirty-one kills with *MFJI*, and Theo Osterkamp, thirty-two victories with *MFJI* and *MFJIII*. Osterkamp also shot down six Allied aircraft in May and July 1940, and became a senior Luftwaffe officer in the Second World War. All three were awarded the Blue Max.

Udet's Black Fokker D.VII whilst commanding *Jasta 4*. The **LO** on the fuselage is for his fiancée, later his wife, Eleonore. His earlier Albatros Scouts carried the same marking.

A new fighter seen over France late in the war was the Pfalz D.VIII. This picture is of the machine flown by **Paul Bäumer** of *Jasta Boelcke*. It carries his red, white and black fuselage stripes. While there were not that many used, it was no doubt often confused in combat by Allied pilots for a Fokker DVII.

Another innovation towards the end of the war was the Fokker E.V, a high-wing monoplane. A few of the aces flew it in combat, especially Theo Osterkamp of *MFJII* who was actually shot down in one in September 1918 by three French Spads and baled out safely.

Third on the list of German aces was Erich Löwenhardt, fifty-four victories. He served with *Jasta 10* of the Richthofen *Geschwader* throughout 1917 and 1918 until his death on 10 August 1918. His Fokker D.VII was shot-up by 56 Squadron and he then collided with another D.VII. Although he took to his parachute it failed to open and he fell to his death.

Top Australian ace in the AFC during the war was Arthur Cobby, from Melbourne. He flew with No. 4 Squadron, Australian Flying Corps in 1918, scoring twenty-nine victories, including five balloons. For this he was awarded the DSO, DFC and two Bars. On his return to Australia he continued to serve with the air force until 1936. In the Second World War he was awarded the George Medal when, as a passenger in a Catalina flying boat which crashed, he was instrumental in saving several other passengers. Post-war he remained in civil aviation, being made a CBE and died on Armistice Day 1955.

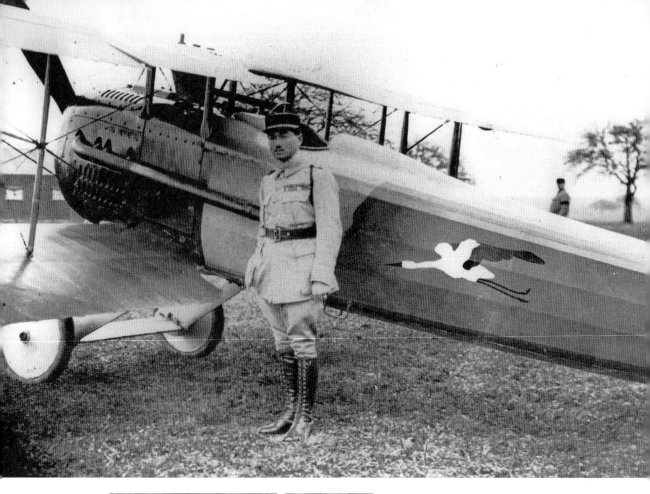

The war's and France's top fighter ace of the First World War, René Fonck, standing by a 'Stork' marked Spad XIII of *Spa103*. He was credited with seventy-five confirmed aerial victories, although he claimed many more either probably destroyed or certainly damaged. He remained in service after the war, becoming Inspector of the French Fighter Force in the 1930s. He died in Paris in June 1953, aged 59.

Another high-scoring Australian was E. J. K. McCloughry, also of 4 Squadron AFC. From Adelaide, he accounted for twenty-one aircraft and balloons during 1918 before being wounded by ground fire. He received the DSO, DFC and Bar and rose to the rank of air vice-marshal in the RAAF, before retiring in 1953. He died in November 1972.

Franz Büchner, from Leipzig, was the son of a wealthy businessman and served in the army in both France and Russia before moving to aviation in 1916. Once a fighter pilot, his achievements were few until he took command of *Jasta 13* in late 1917. During 1918 he began to score regularly and by October his tally reached forty. After the war he flew against the German revolutionaries and was killed by them in March 1918.

Another top Irish ace was Tom Hazell **DSO MC DFC** and Bar. He achieved forty-three victories over aircraft, including ten balloons. His first unit had been the Nieuport-equipped No. 1 Squadron in 1917, but in 1918 he was a flight commander with 24 Squadron. From Galway, he remained in the RAF after the war until retiring in 1927; he died in September 1946, aged fifty-four.